GATHER US IN

TOOLS FOR FORMING FAMILIES

Kathleen O'Connell Chesto, D.Min.

ISBN 978-1-949628-01-2
Printed in the United States of America.
10 9 8 7 6 5 4 3 2 1   22 21 20 19 18

Published by The Pastoral Center, http://pastoral.center.

Copyright © 1999, 2000, 2018 Kathleen O'Connell Chesto.

All rights reserved. Purchase of this book includes a license to reproduce this resource for use in a single parish, school, or other similar organization. You are allowed to share and make unlimited copies only for use within the organization that licensed it. If you serve more than one organization, each should purchase its own license. You may not post this document to any web site without explicit permission to do so. Outside of these conditions, no part of this book may be reproduced in any form or by any means, electronic or mechanical, including photocopying, recording, taping, or via any retrieval system, without the written permission of The Pastoral Center, 1212 Versailles Ave., Alameda, CA 94501. Thank you for cooperating with our honor system regarding our licenses.

For questions or to order additional copies or licenses, please call 1-844-727-8672 or visit http://pastoral.center.

Portions of this work were previously published as *Playing, Learning, Praying: Parish Tools for Gathering Families*; *Rituals & Icebreakers: Practical Tools for Forming Community*; and *FIRE: For the Director*; all published by Liguori Publications.

The Scripture passages contained herein are from the *New Revised Standard Version Bible: Catholic Edition*, copyright © 1989, 1993, by the National Council of the Churches of Christ in the United States of America. Used by permission. All rights reserved.

CONTENTS

INTRODUCTION — 5

PART 1: ICEBREAKERS — 9

A COMMUNITY IS WHERE EVERYONE KNOWS YOUR NAME — 11

Yarn Web — 12
What's My Number? — 13
Noah's Ark — 14
I've Got Your Number — 15
Fact Find — 16
People Bingo — 17

COMMUNITY IS WHERE YOU ARE KNOWN AND LOVED — 19

Gift Find — 20
Hunting for Compliments — 21
Where Do You Stand? — 22
Making a Stronger Stand — 23
Parent-Child Freeze — 24
Statues — 25
Where Are You? — 26
The Orchestra — 27
It Feels like a Gift — 28

A COMMUNITY WORKS TOGETHER — 29

Hidden Treasure — 30
Bumps on a Log — 31
Supporting the Group — 32
Being First Isn't Always Winning — 33
Human Knot — 34
Musical Chairs — 35
Sandman — 36
Button, Button, Who's Got the Button? — 37
More Statues — 38
New Life Scavenger Hunt — 39
Who Am I? — 40
Biblical Time Line — 41
Circle Games — 42
Simon Says — 42

PART 2: SOCIAL & SERVICE IDEAS — 43

Autumn Social Activities — 44
Autumn Service Activities — 46
Advent & Christmas Social Activities — 48
Advent & Christmas Service Activities — 49
Holy Family Sunday — 50
Winter & Lenten Social Activities — 51
Winter & Lenten Service Activities — 53
Easter Season Social Activities — 55
Easter Season Service Activities — 57
Summer Social and Service Activities — 58

PART 3: FAMILY DAY EVENTS — 59

Saints Alive	60
Advent Wreaths	69
Jesse Trees	72
Sacrament Scavenger Hunt	76
Forgiveness	78
Lenten Crosses	81
Calvary Walk	84
Easter Egg Hunt	87
Body of Christ	91
Holy Spirit Kites	96

PART 4: RITUALS & PRAYER SERVICES — 99

A COMMUNITY SHARES SYMBOLS — 101

Symbol Examples	103

A COMMUNITY CELEBRATES RITUALS — 107

Questioning	108
Bread	110
Beauty of Autumn	112
Beginning of the School Year	113
Waiting (Advent)	114
Winter	115
The Desert (Lent)	116
Desert (alternative)	117
New Life (Easter/Spring)	118
Summer Vacation	119

A COMMUNITY'S RITUALS ARE ROOTED IN SYMBOLS — 121

Water	122
Wind	124
Fire	125
Rainbows	126
Time	127
The Cross	128
Circles	129
Stars	131

A COMMUNITY CELEBRATES PRAYER — 133

Celebration of Mercy	134
Holy Spirit Prayer	137

A COMMUNITY COVENANTS TOGETHER — 139

Session on Covenanting and Naming	140
General Covenant Blessing	144
Covenant Celebration	147

BIBLIOGRAPHY — 151

INTRODUCTION

Embracing Parents

The Sunday paper held an interesting story on a plan to improve academic achievement in "Title One" schools throughout Connecticut. The new federal grant money was not being spent on computers, or texts, or tutors, or "motivational equipment." The money had been allotted to provide "family activity days," school-sponsored afternoons of family activities. Contemporary educational research has revealed that one of the greatest predictors of academic success is parental involvement.

How much more true is this of the faith! The Church's emphasis on an adult catechesis as the norm reflects not only the adult nature of belief, but the simple fact that parental faith is one of the strongest indicators of childhood and later adult faith. However, that focus on the adult assumes an interaction between parent and child that allows the child to become acquainted with the faith of the parent. Too often, that interaction is simply not happening.

Parishes throughout the country are attempting to rectify the situation much the same way as the State School Board in Connecticut. We are organizing activities—social, educational, and service—that allow families to work and play together while sharing and living out their faith. This book is meant as an aid in that process. Any parish wishing to make faith more meaningful for its families and also hoping to foster strong family life, will find help in these pages.

Forming True Community

The hunger for community is an overwhelming feature of today's society. We gather in groups that promise to "support" us in anything from losing weight to dealing with death. There is a support group somewhere for every ache expressed by the human spirit and some for those we have yet to voice. In asking group after group around the North American continent what they hope for from their churches, the first response I receive is always "community."

Yet, I have found very few churches that actually succeed in becoming community. Part of the problem is often size; it is difficult to be community where no one knows your name. Part of the problem rests with the individuals who want community to miraculously happen to them, without the struggle and the pain that true community always involves. And part of the problem is the rugged individualism so much a part of the American spirit, an individualism that tells us we should be able to do everything on our own. Becoming a community implies being vulnerable, and many of us are simply not willing to take that risk.

According to M. Scott Peck, community is a group of individuals who have learned how to communicate honestly with each other, whose relationships go deeper than their masks of composure, who have developed some significant commitment to rejoice together, mourn together, delight in each other. Such a community is inherently mysterious, a whole that is more than the sum of its parts, people drawn together by crisis, common need, a shared moment, or perhaps just by chance.[1]

Most churches of several hundred families have already discovered that becoming a community with "significant commitment" and "deeper relationships" requires starting with small groups within which these relationships are possible. Our first community was a small group of families, drawn together by "common need," the need to hand on our faith tradition to our children in an environment that supported that faith, with people who shared our moral and spiritual commitment. We discovered that even an intense devotion to a common task is not enough to create a community. Communities may be drawn together by accident or chance; they take time and attention to survive and grow.

The religious education program that grew out of that first group of families, has been struggling for decades to help other families develop support communities for handing on faith. This book is not intended as a treatise on community-building or an exploration of the phases a group passes through on its way to becoming community. It is a simple effort to provide groups, particularly those with a wide span of ages, with tools we have discovered were necessary in developing certain aspects of community. None of the games, rituals or activities, and no amount of strict adherence to playing and praying, will "create" community, any more than flour and eggs can create a cake. These ingredients are offered with the hope of making the group's task easier as it struggles to become community.

Tools for Gathering Families

The book is divided into four sections. The first section offers *icebreakers*: games for learning names, games for getting to know one another better, games for learning to work and play together. These games have been used successfully with Scouts, PTA's, youth ministry programs, 4-H, and various catechetical programs and retreats.

The second section is made up of simple ideas and suggestions for *social and service activities*. Many are germs of ideas meant to jumpstart a brainstorming process in your own parish on how you can provide opportunities for families to play with one another, and to reach out in service to their communities.

These activities are divided according to the seasons of the year. I have begun with autumn in the simple acknowledgment of the fact that the lives of most families are governed by the school year, not the liturgical year, and parish plans need to be made accordingly.

Service activities are most successful when everyone is able to contribute and recognizes his or her contribution as valuable. Choose service activities that fit both your families and your community, and provide ways for everyone to participate. While service activities invite us to stretch a little

---

[1] M. Scott Peck. *The Different Drum* (New York: Simon and Schuster, 1987).

beyond our usual limits, do not enter into projects that make the majority of people uncomfortable. The aim of fostering large group service activities is to enable families to discover the joy and the fun involved in giving, especially in the company of others.

The third section of the book contains "*family days*" that are not really "days" but activities approximately two to three hours in length. In "family days," an idea is worked out completely for the coordinator. The time and materials needed, the purpose of the activity, the appropriate season, directions for the experience and any prayer involved, are all clearly explained. These activities can be done as they are presented, combined with service and social ideas from the second section, or rounded out with prayer experiences from the final section.

The fourth section contains *rituals, prayer services, and tools* for forming and celebrating Covenants. It begins with a reflection on the use of symbol in the development of ritual prayer and directions for making and using specific symbols within a group. The remainder of the section is comprised of rituals, divided into four sets. Rituals in the first set celebrate general themes, seasons, and ideas, with directions for using a concrete symbol. The second set of rituals focuses on the more specific themes represented by the symbols described earlier and are cross-referenced with these symbols for easier use. The third set offers more extensive prayer services. The final set includes sessions and prayer experiences to help groups develop, commit to, and celebrate a Covenant. While many of the rituals were designed for beginning and closing meetings or classes, most can be expanded into prayer services that stand alone.

Leading Your Community

Parents are the primary educators of their children. Nothing done in or "by" the parish is capable of influencing children as much as the faith life of their parents. It seems only reasonable then, as parishes, that we dedicate more effort to shaping that faith life and providing the opportunities when it can be shared. If we make those opportunities fun as well as meaningful, families will want to participate. In the end, we will not only be fostering a stronger faith community, we will be building stronger families.

Involve families who are not already in leadership roles in planning your activities and events, and issue special invitations to the teens to assist. The more people involved in planning a process, the more successful it will be.

What we discovered in leading family catechesis was that the heart of the lesson is never the experience, the feedback, or the prayer; it is the community. If we neglected to develop that community, we were limited to a religious education program that teaches doctrine to families. To neglect to develop community in any group that meets within our churches, from youth ministry programs to adult education, is to limit that group to accomplishing a task and to deprive it of a potential experience of church.

PART 1
ICEBREAKERS

Every group that gathers brings with it its own fears and prejudices. There is a tendency for new group members to enter with their guard up, seeing themselves as separate and different from the others, sitting in judgment, to some extent, on the personhood of others. Before anything of strong lasting value can take place, some of those walls need to be broken down.

This is the process of "icebreaking." It is an excellent word because the image it conveys is exactly what we are trying to accomplish. Icebreakers chop through the hardened surface of built-in fears and frozen misconceptions. First they leave the chunks of ice free to bump up against one another, wear down some of the rougher edges, and even exchange places in the water. Eventually, enough of the ice is broken into small enough chunks to allow the water to flow freely, carrying the remaining ice flows away in the flood.

The more resistant a group is to icebreakers, the more in need they are of the process.

A COMMUNITY IS WHERE EVERYONE KNOWS YOUR NAME

A community is where everyone knows your name. Being called by name empowers us. You are not "one of the Smith's"; you are "Emily," unique, different, special. Scripture tells us over and over again the importance of name. Isaiah says: "I have called you by name and you are mine" (Is. 43:1b). Calling someone by name implies a connectedness, a belonging to one another. Any group that hopes to become a community needs to pay careful attention to this fact and be willing to devote the time it takes to get to know everyone by name.

Of equal importance is naming the group. A group that has no name will always be known by the leader's name, as in "I belong to Kathy Chesto's group." Simply by making such a statement, the speaker places the responsibility and ownership for the group solely on the leader's shoulders. By naming the group, and allowing everyone some voice in choosing the name, the responsibility is extended to the group as a whole. The name can be as simple as a number or Greek letter, or as complex as a scripture reference. I have been in parishes where all the groups in a renewal program were numbered, and I have heard community names as varied as "Voyagers," "Fireworks," "Beehive," and "Happiness Is…." "I belong to the Beehive" carries in the very statement a sense of ownership missing when we name a group by the leader.

Naming a group involves the struggle to understand the meaning and purpose this community has for those within it. It is a symbolic act of assigning significance to a group that may not, as yet, have experienced its own significance. Owning the name usually proves to be a far longer process than simply designating it.

The task of learning members' names is less complex but often more demanding. It requires attentiveness. Creating an atmosphere where everyone is free to call each person by name also involves vulnerability and risk.

The following games are designed for learning—and remembering!—names. Some of them may seem silly, and adults may, at first, feel foolish playing them. They are a leveling force in any community, asking us to be willing to risk surrendering a little of our self-assurance in order to be truly known by others. All of them can be played several times, and most are more enjoyable the second or third time through.

Don't be afraid to spend several weeks learning names. Most people will be grateful to be reminded. Adults have a particularly difficult time with the names of children because our society allows them to be dismissed as lesser members of a family. Knowing everyone's name will not make a group into a community, but not knowing names will certainly prevent a group from becoming one.

YARN WEB

GROUP SIZE

10-40. The game is uninteresting with too small a group, and boring and cumbersome with too large a group.

GROUP AGE

Intergenerational

MATERIALS

- A large ball of yarn

PURPOSE

Learning names

DIRECTIONS

The leader begins holding a large ball of yarn. The leader says her name and something she particularly likes that begins with the same sound. For example, "My name is Kathy and I like cookies." It is important to use the same sound rather than the same letter, since younger children in the group will not know how to spell.

As the leader speaks, she grasps the end of the yarn and throws the ball to someone else in the group. The second person grabs the yarn, pulling it taut with the leader, gives his name and something he likes that begins with the same sound, and tosses the yarn ball to someone else.

The game continues until everyone has been thrown the ball and is holding a piece of the yarn. (It is necessary to remind people frequently before they throw the ball, to hold on to the yarn.) The yarn will form a web across the center of the group.

The leader should then tug on the yarn, demonstrating that everyone can feel the pull. In a community, what affects one of us affects all of us. The web is distorted if any member drops an end, but the community can still support it.

If there is extra time, the community can try to unweave the web by having the last person throw the yarn ball back to the person from whom it was caught, naming the person and what she likes. This is far more difficult than it sounds: the yarn can get badly tangled if the ball drops, but it can be fun!

When the group knows names a little better, the game can be repeated, having the person who throws the ball name the person to whom it is thrown.

WHAT'S MY NUMBER?

GROUP SIZE

10 or more. (The larger the group, the longer the game can go on.)

GROUP AGE

This can be done with anyone old enough to write, or with intergenerational groups having younger members by pairing those children with an adult.

MATERIALS

- Slips of paper, each containing a different number, enough for each person in the group to have one
- Common pins
- Paper and pencils

PURPOSE

Learning names

DIRECTIONS

As each person enters the meeting, the leader and one or two helpers pin a number on the person's back. Each person also receives a pencil and paper. Ask people to sit immediately, so they are not revealing their numbers before they know how to play the game.

The idea of the game is to find out everyone's number while not revealing your own. When a participant sees a person's number, he writes the person's name and number on the slip of paper. If the participant is not old enough to write, she can work in partnership with an adult, as long as she is old enough to recognize numerals. Children are actually very good at sneaking behind people and discovering numbers. However, it is not fair to carry a child piggyback with the intent of hiding the bearer's number.

Once the rules have been explained, ask everyone to stand up and "mill about," trying to keep their numbers secret. They are allowed to pair up with someone, if they choose to do so. Allow about 10 minutes for the game. Participants must ask members' names if they don't know them. The person who has the most correct names and numbers on her list wins.

Don't be surprised if the less-competitive in the group make no effort to win, or focus on helping a child. The idea is to have fun and learn people's names. Any way that works for the group is fine.

Teens are particularly fond of this game and will play longer and more intensely than a group of mixed ages. They will have fun with it long after they know everyone's name.

NOAH'S ARK

GROUP SIZE

10-50. You are actually only limited by the number of animals you can name. You can play the game in groups, instead of pairs, if you run out of animals.

GROUP AGE

Intergenerational

MATERIALS

- One index card for each person in the group, the name of an animal on each card. Every animal must appear on two cards if you are playing in pairs, or on several cards if you have over 50 people and you are playing in large groups.

PURPOSE

Having fun, learning names

DIRECTIONS (PLAYING IN PAIRS)

As each person comes in, give her a card with an animal name on it and ask her to keep it a secret. Make SURE that you have two of each animal. If you have an odd number of people in your group, the leader should balance it off by playing or not playing, as needed. Try to make sure that people in the same family do not get the same animal. It is also possible to hand the names out just before you begin to play. Designate an area of the room as Noah's Ark.

Instruct everyone to make a noise or a motion, or both, to indicate the animal each has. All must get up and move around the room doing this until they find their partner animals. Once they find their partners, they go and stand in Noah's Ark and continue to make the noise or motion. When everyone is in the ark, talk briefly about how cramped and smelly it must have gotten after 40 days. Everyone was anxious to get off.

To leave the ark, members must be able to introduce each other to the group. They leave together and go sit down.

FOR GROUP PLAYING

In large groups, give several people the names of the same animal. They must begin to make noise. As they find their like animals, they continue to move through the group, collecting all the dogs, cats, pigs, or whatever. When they are certain that all have been found, they move to the side of the room and continue to make their noise. The object is to finish first and have fun, making enough noise to confuse the others.

This variation works best in a large parish hall.

I'VE GOT YOUR NUMBER

GROUP SIZE

16-50. There must be an even number of people. The leader should play or not play, as needed.

GROUP AGE

Intergenerational

MATERIALS

- A small piece of paper for each person in the group. One numeral is written on each paper, each numeral is written twice.

PURPOSE

Getting to know each other better

DIRECTIONS

Before the group arrives, the leader chooses a fact she wants the people of the group to learn about each other. If the group is fairly new, choose something simple such as: favorite color, favorite music, favorite sport, worst food, etc. Each person is given a number as he enters. There are two of each numeral. Make sure people in the same family do not get matching numbers. The object is to find the other person with your number. However, before you are allowed to ask anyone her number, you must first ask the person's name and the particular fact decided in advance by the leader. As soon as the match is made, both people sit down. When everyone is sitting, pairs introduce each other to the group and give the person's response to the "favorite" question.

If your group has been meeting for some time and you are certain that all the names are known, you can ask a tougher question, such as "Name one thing that really makes you angry," before you ask the person's number. This information can then be shared with the group. Do not, however, assume prematurely that all names are known.

FACT FIND

GROUP SIZE

15+

GROUP AGE

Members need to be able to read. In intergenerational groups, small children or those who have difficulty reading can be partnered with parents or other adults. Or the game can be played in teams.

MATERIALS

- A list of 20 facts for each person. People should all be given the same list, with a space for writing a name after each fact, e.g.,
  - Hates chocolate_____
  - Got an A in math_____
  - Likes country music_____
  - Has a cat_____
  - Can't swim_____
  - Plays flute_____
  - Favorite meal is breakfast_____
  - Watches "The Voice"_____
  - etc. (Include things specific to your group.)

PURPOSE

Learning names, getting to know each other better

DIRECTIONS

Everyone is given a list of facts as the meeting begins. The object of the game is to find a person who fits each fact. Each person may only be used once. The group is given 5-7 minutes to find the right people. Time is called before anyone gets all 20. The person who was able to match the most items wins. Be sure to check for accuracy by having the winner read facts and names aloud. If there are teenagers, have a prize that can be shared by the family, like a gift certificate for hamburgers or pizza.

PEOPLE BINGO

GROUP SIZE

15+ (This has been done successfully with several hundred people.)

GROUP AGE

This game also requires reading ability, but little ones can be teamed with adults. This game also works well with adults only.

MATERIALS

- Bingo cards for each person (sample given below) Pencils

PURPOSE

Learning names, getting to know people better

DIRECTIONS

The object of the game is to get "Bingo," i.e., to fill in people to match the squares in horizontal, vertical or diagonal column. No name may be used more than once in a winning row. The game can be played with all the cards alike, with different facts on each person's card, or with the same facts in different order on the cards. Be creative and make your own cards. It is important when someone shouts "Bingo" to have that person read the names and facts in the winning row.

This game can be made more challenging if people are not allowed to ask questions that require "yes" or "no" answers. If a fact is "loves cats," the person attempting to fill the blank may not ask "Do you like cats?" but will have to ask, "What pets do you love?", etc. Played this way, the game takes a little longer.

B	I	N	G	O
likes history	plays soccer	was in a play	plays piano	middle name is John
ran for office	won a trophy	remembers dreams	sings in the shower	hates pizza
reads mysteries	goes to college	has never been on a train	likes nail polish	uses an electric shaver
was born in fall	likes peanut butter	has been in a foreign country	collects something (e.g. stamps)	has never broken a bone
owns a teddy bear	takes dancing lessons	likes to jump rope	saves money	has flown a kite this year

COMMUNITY IS WHERE YOU ARE KNOWN AND LOVED

There is an old saying "A friend is someone who knows you as you are and loves you anyway." Knowing is the beginning of friendship and the reason we stress knowing names. But for community to develop, we must know more about people than their names, and we must be able to demonstrate that we love and support them "anyway." "In community, instead of being ignored, denied, hidden, or changed, human differences are celebrated as gifts."[2]

The following games are designed to lead a group into a slightly deeper knowledge of each other. Many of them can be modified to ask more in-depth questions of a group that has already bonded as a community. Community is something that can never be taken for granted. Because you have established the first step well does not mean it no longer needs attention. Communities are like plants: they need sunshine, food, and water to grow. It is easy to rush into the lesson, once a group has become a community, but it will not remain a community without nurturing.

---

2 M. Scott Peck. *The Different Drum* (New York: Simon and Schuster, 1987), p.62.

GIFT FIND

GROUP SIZE

Any number

GROUP AGE

The ability to read on a second to third grade level is needed for this game. It can be done with an intergenerational group by pairing the young children with adults or teens.

MATERIALS

- Lists of gifts (given below)
- Pencils for all

PURPOSE

Getting to know people better, affirmation

LIST OF GIFTS

My best gift is… .

1. friendliness _____
2. strength _____
3. neatness _____
4. gentleness _____
5. mechanical ability (fixing things) _____
6. promptness (being on time) _____
7. leadership _____
8. athletics _____
9. coloring _____
10. helpfulness _____
11. singing _____
12. cheerfulness _____
13. schoolwork _____
14. listening _____
15. organization _____
16. playing a musical instrument _____
17. dancing _____
18. carpooling _____
19. creativity _____
20. remembering _____
21. math _____
22. writing _____
23. perseverance (sticking to things) _____
24. being observant (noticing things) _____
25. sensitivity _____
26. honesty _____

It would be helpful for leaders to take careful note of the people in the group and make out these lists of gifts to fit the qualities they have seen. The generic list will work, though.

DIRECTIONS

At the start of the game, give people the lists and ask them to read through the qualities, helping younger members with hard words. Ask all members to choose which quality on the list they think is their best quality. Encourage parents to help little ones to decide. At a signal, everyone gets up and moves about, asking other group members their gift. The object of the game is to fill as many of the blank spaces as possible. Two names in the same space does not count. People may not *change* their gift to help out.

The person who fills the most blanks in five minutes wins. You may want to extend the time if it takes the group a little while to warm up.

A variation to this game can be played by having group members choose the people in whom they see a particular gift. Before they can write the name in the blank, though, they must approach the person and explain why they see this person as having a particular gift.

HUNTING FOR COMPLIMENTS

GROUP SIZE

Any size.

GROUP AGE

This game can be played by anyone old enough to speak, but children between the ages of 8 and 13 are often uncomfortable pointing out good things in others. Little ones will need help writing names and can be paired with an adult.

MATERIALS

- Paper and pencil for everyone

PURPOSE

Affirmation

DIRECTIONS

This hunt also involves finding good things in others. The object of the game is to sincerely compliment as many people in the group as possible. Each person starts off with a blank sheet of paper and approaches someone in the group and points out a good quality he has noticed in that person. It must be a sincere, *meaningful* compliment, not "I like your shirt!" The complimented person signs her name to the complimenter's list. Little ones can participate by being paired with a parent and they are frequently quite adept at noticing good things in others. Their compliments can be honest and moving.

The leader allows a specified time (10 minutes works well), then calls the game to a halt. The leader checks for the person with the longest list of complimented people. Before she is declared a winner, she must read the name of each person and share with the group the compliment that was given to that person. The group may disqualify any remarks not considered true compliments and declare a new winner.

WHERE DO YOU STAND?

GROUP SIZE

10-40—larger if you are working in a large space.

GROUP AGE

Old enough to understand the statements and walk. The age level will vary with statements used.

MATERIALS

- An open space to use for a continuum walk
- Words prepared in advance by the leader
- Three signs reading: LOVE, HATE, NO OPINION

PURPOSE

To review names in a group where people know each other, to understand the members of the group better, to ask people to practice "making a stand" for what they believe

DIRECTIONS

Tell the group that you are going to ask them to take a stand on how they feel about certain things. If you stand by the left wall, it means you absolutely love something. (Put the sign LOVE on the wall and demonstrate by standing near it.) If you hate it, you will walk to the right wall. (Put the sign HATE on the right wall.) If you have no preference, stand in the middle. Put the sign NO OPINION on the floor in the middle. Give an example. State "peanut butter" and demonstrate the different places you might stand if you love it, like it, don't care, dislike it, or hate it. Make sure the directions are understood by small children and reassure them that they can ask for help if they get confused. They may have difficulty remembering which wall means which and need to be reminded by whomever is standing near them at the moment. It is important for the group to notice where other people are standing, because when the activity is over, you are going to ask them "Who likes peanut butter?", etc.

Choose several simple things for the continuum. Suggestions: pizza, school, roller coasters, homework, country music, skiing, rock music, baseball, math, chocolate, singing, ice cream, reading, hats, baked beans, spaghetti, merry-go-rounds, television, football, soap operas, talking on the telephone, cookies, mittens, bubbles, science, finger paints, etc. Your choices will depend on the ages of the "people in your group. As you read a word, everyone goes to stand in a spot which indicates his feeling about that particular thing. Continue playing for about seven minutes, or until you feel you are losing the group's interest. Ask the group to sit down.

Ask if anyone can tell you someone (other than herself) who loved skiing, who hated peanut butter, who liked science, etc. Little ones will want to tell you that they like or hate the thing you mentioned. Ask them if anyone else in the group was standing with them at that moment because that person feels the same way they do. This helps to keep the game focused, while acknowledging what the young children will want to say. It provides a way to review names, while offering some miscellaneous information about the people in the group.

MAKING A STRONGER STAND

GROUP SIZE

10-40, depending on the size of the space in which the game is played.

GROUP AGE

Intergenerational; little ones will need help

MATERIALS

- List of controversial statements prepared in advance by the leader
- Signs reading: Agree, Disagree, No Opinion

PURPOSE

To invite members to "make a stand," to get to know people's values a little better

DIRECTIONS

This game is played in the same way as the former continuum, but it is for groups who know each other a little better and have developed a rudimentary level of trust. Once again, set up the continuum with AGREE on the left wall, DISAGREE on the right wall, and NO OPINION on the floor in the middle. The group is allowed to talk to each other as they are making their decisions where to stand. (If the group has become fairly relaxed, older ones will try to convince little ones to "come to their side." The leader can encourage this by joining in the game and trying to talk others into joining her in her opinion.)

The reader begins by reading phrases, more value-laden than the words of the earlier game. While these statements are better prepared by a leader who knows her group, some suggestions are given here:

- Adults should be seen and not heard.
- People are at their most creative when they are teens.
- Running is the best way to stay in shape.
- Swimming is the healthiest form of exercise.
- Video stores should not allow children under 17 to rent R-rated videos.
- Children should get an allowance.
- Parents should be responsible for anything their children do.
- People under 16 should be allowed to drive.
- Grandparents make the best babysitters.
- Children should get rewards for good grades.
- There is too much violence in movies.
- Grown-ups watch too much television/video.

Try to fit the statements to the ages and interests in your group. Don't make them too controversial. It is not necessary to do the feedback on names when the game is played this way. The principal point here is to allow people to express their feelings. The game is played the same way as the previous continuum "Make a Stand."

Once you have played this game, as various issues come up in the group, tell everyone you will add them to the continuum list and use the newly compiled list again at a later date.

This game can be used to express feelings about the actions of Biblical characters: "Jacob was wrong to trick Esau." The great value of the walking continuum is that it gives people a chance to practice taking a deliberate stand in 'the view of others for what they believe in, even if it is only liking baked beans when everyone else hates them. All of us need practice in recognizing we can think very differently from others and still be respected.

PARENT-CHILD FREEZE

GROUP SIZE

15-40. This can be done in larger groups when all participants are over 10 and able to watch and enjoy when they are not actively involved.

GROUP AGE

Intergenerational

MATERIALS

- A large adult shoe
- A small children's shoe

PURPOSE

To help members understand each other better, to foster parent-child communication

DIRECTIONS

Ask an adult and child to volunteer for the game. Prepare an argument in advance with the two people chosen to help. Any parent/child issue will do: cleaning your room, staying up late to watch videos, etc., anything a parent and child argue about. Ask the child to assume the parent role (and give the child the large shoe to hold), and the parent the child role (and the small shoe). Tell the group that they are about to eavesdrop on a parent/child argument. They will know which person is being the parent in the argument because the parent will be the person holding the big shoe, the child will hold the little one. Move the two people who have been prepared to the center of the group. Let them begin to argue. Once all understand what the argument is about and who is playing which part (ask the group to allow at least two minutes), any person in the group can call FREEZE, go to the center and take either shoe, and continue the argument from the adult perspective, if they have taken the large shoe, or from the child's perspective, if they have taken the small one. It takes a group a few minutes to want to participate in this activity, but then the problem becomes giving each person who jumps in enough time to do or say something. Encourage people, if they can, to take the role they do NOT have in the family.

Once this game is learned as an icebreaker, it can later be used in discussions of moral issues that are impacting the life of the group. As it becomes more familiar, children and adults will introduce topics into the argument that they nave been afraid to discuss at home. It is important to remain nonjudgmental and to keep the tone light. This is not group therapy; it is a tool to enable discussion.

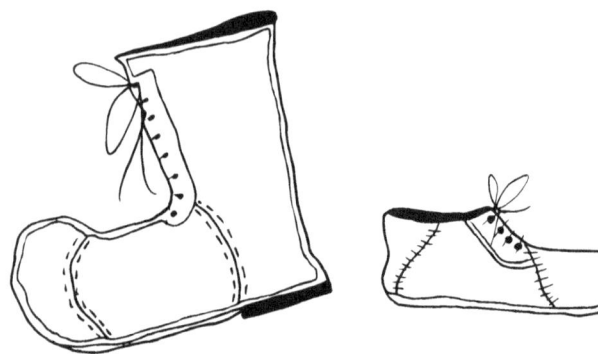

STATUES

GROUP SIZE

5-10 families. (This activity is specifically for families. It can be done in large groups, but it becomes time consuming.)

GROUP AGE

Intergenerational

MATERIALS

▶ None

PURPOSE

To help families understand themselves better and to share who they are with the group.

DIRECTIONS

Ask the group if any of them have seen the statue "The Thinker" by Rodin. Someone in the group probably has. Ask that person to demonstrate how the statue is posed. If no one in the group knows, demonstrate yourself, sitting with knees slightly spread apart, elbow on knee, chin resting on the hand. The person in the statue really looks like he is thinking. It is possible, in a statue, to capture an action like thinking or a quality like thoughtfulness.

Ask each family to come up with what they feel is their outstanding *positive* trait. It is important to stress the positive part. Ask the family to figure out a way to create a statue, using their own bodies, that will demonstrate that trait. Give the families some separate space to work in (it doesn't need to be a separate room, just a little area) and allow 5-10 minutes (depending on how quickly they appear to be accomplishing the task). This activity moves more quickly with families with only young children since the adults do not have to discuss and tend to take control. Move among the families and make sure the children are being heard, Singles in a group can create their own statues or help leaders.

Bring the families back and allow them, one at a time, to share their statues. The group can guess the outstanding trait they are trying to demonstrate.

This activity can be modified to express actions that the family enjoys doing together, like roasting marshmallows around a campfire, or things they do together but dislike, like laundry or yard work.

WHERE ARE YOU?

GROUP SIZE

10-25 people

GROUP AGE

Teen to adult

MATERIALS

- A writing surface, such as a chalk board or easel, and chalk or marker

PURPOSE

To become more present to the group and the activity at hand

DIRECTIONS

Begin by writing on the surface the percentage of yourself that is actually present to the group. Explain. It may be that only 60% of you is present because 20% of you is at the office, 5% with the soccer game you didn't get to see, 10% with the homework you were trying to help your son do, and 5% of you is just missing. It got mislaid in the rush to get to the meeting. Invite others to share by writing their percentage on the board.

This can be a long warm-up because people often have several things to say. Encourage them to be brief. Enumerating the things often helps us to let go of them and be truly present. This is especially good for meetings where only the adults may be present.

The game can be played more simply (to include younger children) by asking which part of your body is here and which part is not and why. The heart may be in the meeting, but the head may be back with the math assignment.

THE ORCHESTRA

GROUP SIZE

10-35—(too many people can make this unwieldy)

GROUP AGE

Intergenerational

MATERIALS

- Pencil and paper for each family
- Names of each family in the group on separate sheets of paper.

PURPOSE

Affirmation

DIRECTIONS

Put the slips of paper with the family names in a dish. Instruct the families that they will be working together as a family for this activity. Single-person households need to work alone for this activity.

Each family (household) draws a slip of paper from the dish. If they draw their own name, they should put it back and draw again. The family is to consider the family they have drawn. If the group were an orchestra, what instrument would each member of that family be playing, and why?

Give people enough time to assign instruments, then call them back to the group. The game can be made more interesting for little ones by having pictures of instruments, drawn or cut from catalogs, to put people's names on. Let one family at a time present to the family they drew the instruments they see them as being. They should say each person's name and explain why that person is the violin, piano, etc., for the group.

This activity really needs to end with a song. In groups with many small children, everyone can be encouraged to "play" their instrument for the song. (Middle-schoolers will absolutely refuse to do anything that corny.)

IT FEELS LIKE A GIFT

GROUP SIZE

10-25—too many more people would take too long.

GROUP AGE

Intergenerational, but small children will need help.

MATERIALS

- "It feels like a gift" cards, enough for every person, samples given here.

PURPOSE

To recognize the everyday gifts we give to one another.

Sample cards:

- Helping feels like a gift when…
- Listening feels like a gift when…
- A visit feels like a gift when…
- A phone call feels like a gift when…
- A loan feels like a gift when…
- Flowers feel like a gift when…
- An invitation feels like a gift when…
- Forgiveness feels like a gift when…
- Sharing feels like a gift when…
- Caring feels like a gift when…
- Friendship feels like a gift when…
- A letter feels like a gift when…
- A compliment feels like a gift when…
- A photograph feels like a gift when…
- A meal feels like a gift when…
- A friend feels like a gift when…
- Acceptance feels like a gift when…
- A smile feels like a gift when…
- A touch feels like a gift when…
- Tears feel like a gift when…
- Rain feels like a gift when…
- Sunshine feels like a gift when…

DIRECTIONS

The object of this game is to help the community to understand that all gifts don't come in packages with pretty wrappings. Some of the best gifts are the ones we give each other every day.

Ask each person in the group to take a card and think about a time when someone gave them the gift written on it, or when they gave the gift to someone. The more specific they can be, the better. For example, "A compliment feels like a gift when I've studied real hard for a test and the teacher says it shows, like yesterday in math." Young children will need a parent or others to read their cards to them and to help them choose situations. Don't be afraid to let them share. They are often more capable of recognizing the gift in the ordinary.

A COMMUNITY WORKS TOGETHER

An important part of being community is the ability to work together. It isn't enough to know one another's names und to care about each other. We also need to be able to look outward together, to care together about something beyond us.

Intergenerational communities take the longest of any form of community to learn to work together. Adults frequently begin by believing they are only "there for the kids," pushing the children forward in each situation, whispering suggestions in their ears, instead of volunteering themselves. Once the adults get caught up in the situation, though, they run the risk of taking over. How many boxcar derbies have we seen with cars built by adult men screaming at each other while bewildered Cub Scouts stood by, or 4-H fashion shows with clothes clearly made by mothers! (My comparisons here are sexist; unfortunately, they reflect he reality of many of these events.) Adults have little experience of working with children outside of home situations, and the home and yard cleaning and repair that once provided that opportunity is fast disappearing.

These games are an attempt to offer adults and children fun ways to work together. There may be problems to be solved, races to be won, etc. The competition is not the key here. The important issue is the cooperation.

Groups of like ages also benefit from games that prepare them for more serious work together. The game helps develop a cooperation mind-set before the work actually begins. Frequently, what is most needed in a group is the ability to have fun together. Remember to take Time to Play.

HIDDEN TREASURE

GROUP SIZE

12-32 people in four teams. The game can accommodate more people by breaking into more teams, but eight on a team is the real limit for having everyone involved.

GROUP AGES

Intergenerational

MATERIALS

- Paper bag for each team
- Lists of hidden treasures (sample given below)

PURPOSE

Learning to function as a team

Sample list:

fork	earbuds	picture	newspaper
glasses	sweater	sneaker	sheet music
blush	whistle	Bible	cough drop
license	eraser	ticket	checkbook
stub	scarf	candle	envelope
battery	lollipop	pen	stopwatch
souvenir	flower	trophy	1966 penny
pencil	lipstick	marbles	acorn
matches			

DIRECTIONS

The leader needs to prepare by deciding how many teams will be needed and making a list for each team. The lists can be the same or different, but should be equally difficult. The list given here is simply a sample, and longer than your lists need to be. Choose things you know have a chance of being available in the area, on people, in purses, pockets, etc.

Divide the group into teams and let them discuss the list. Decide how much time will be allowed—the more people on a team, the less time they should be given. Do not allow enough time for any team to find all the articles. If you want to use the game as a simple warm-up, make the lists short, but not so short any team will find everything. When the command is given, everyone scrambles to find the articles.

All members of the team will need to work together. If you are working with families, split them up. This adds to the fun, since children will go to their parents on other teams to try to con them out of articles they know they are carrying. If you decide to divide the groups up by age, be careful about your choice of articles, since children would be disadvantaged by many of the articles on the sample list given.

The winning team is the one that comes up with the greatest number of *legitimate* articles. Allow time in your planning for people to share the articles they have found, since some are likely to be quite creative.

BUMPS ON A LOG

GROUP SIZE

10-16, or teams of 10-16 people

GROUP AGE

Intergenerational

MATERIALS

- A log for each team, long enough to support the number of people on the team. A 2x4 or 2x6 (if you want it to be easier) can take the place of the log.
- This game needs to be played in a large room with a floor that can support these logs, or played outside.

PURPOSE

Reviewing names, working together

DIRECTIONS

If you have more than 16 people in your group, split into teams. It is important to have at least eight people on a team for the game to be fun. Show each team their "log" and invite them to go and stand on it.

Once all members are standing on the log, ask them to get into alphabetical order by first names, without ever stepping off the log! The idea is for every team to succeed in doing this, not to compete to do it first. Little ones can crawl under people's legs and are very handy to have on your log. They will need to be reminded to stay on the log (but it does not count if they forget). Once a group has completed the task, they should sound off, people shouting their names in order. The group is free to decide which end of the log will be the "A" and which end the "Z".

This game can be played again at a later date by changing the ordering. Once people see the logs again, they will make sure they get on them alphabetically. Try having them arrange themselves by birthdates, with January as the starting point. Last names can also work, if you are not dealing with families.

SUPPORTING THE GROUP

GROUP SIZE

Any size divided into teams of 8-10 people

GROUP AGE

Intergenerational

MATERIALS

- A telephone book (or other sturdy object of similar size) for each team

PURPOSE

Group problem-solving

DIRECTIONS

Give each group a telephone book and a space to work where they will not be in the direct line of vision of the other groups. Instruct the groups:

"The object of this activity is to have everyone in the group supported by the telephone book (just as we are all supported by the Bible). Arrange yourselves in such a way that everyone in the group is supported by one foot on the book. The other foot *may not* be touching the floor."

How you word your directions is important. By not instructing the group to "stand on" the book, some may find other, creative ways of doing the exercise. Tell the groups to come back and sit down as soon as they are ready to demonstrate to others how they have solved the problem. Do not give them more than 5-7 minutes. Have everyone demonstrate the group's solutions.

BEING FIRST ISN'T ALWAYS WINNING

GROUP SIZE

Any size

GROUP AGE

Intergenerational. This game works best with people of very different ages and sizes.

MATERIALS

- Several pieces of rope, one for every two people in the group.
- Outside space (this is an OUTSIDE game).

PURPOSE

Cooperation

DIRECTIONS

This is a race that is not what it appears to be. Mark an area outside as the starting and finish line. If the course meanders at all, mark that. This is best played on a grassy surface so that no one gets hurt.

Begin by choosing two judges. They can be asked in advance and should be people in the group who may not be comfortable running, or may not be able to run. If you have several people in this category, place them at strategic points along the track. Tell your judges *only* that they will be judging *not* who runs the fastest, but who works together the best. This may be the fastest couple, but it may not.

Pair everyone else off. You may want to choose pairs or allow them to choose their own. Ask tall people to team up with small ones, since they will need help. The judges should be watching the early stages for signs of cooperation.

Once everyone has a partner, instruct the partners to tie their legs together at the ankles (three-legged race style) and line up at the starting line. When you give the signal, they are to run as fast and as *carefully* as they can to the finish. Tell the group that the most important thing is to work with your partner. Some may hear this and catch on, others will just want to race.

Run the race. At the end of the race, tell everyone the judges are going to convene to decide the winners. Give the judges a few minutes, then let them pronounce the "winners" with an explanation of why they won. There can be as many winners as there are people really trying to work together. You may want to name first, second, and third places.

Competition is not necessarily bad. It becomes bad when our total focus is on beating others. We can win by cooperation, and sometimes that even wins the race.

HUMAN KNOT

GROUP SIZE

10-20, or teams of 10 to 20

GROUP AGE

This game is difficult to play with people who vary too much in size. While it is something children over three can understand and do, you may want to put them in a separate group from the 12+ because the size difference will be difficult.

MATERIALS

▶ None

PURPOSE

Working together, reviewing names

DIRECTIONS

Invite the group to stand in a circle facing the center, or in two circles to accommodate very different sizes or large numbers. Everyone joins hands. The leader begins by saying "My right hand is holding N...'s left hand." Each person in the group states whose left hand is in his right hand and carefully remembers this person. If there is more than one group, do this announcing separately, not simultaneously. Instruct everyone to drop hands and have people take different positions in the circle, *without* joining hands. *Remaining in their new positions*, members take the *same* left hand that was *originally* in their right hands. This will involve reaching across the group, etc., and all hands should be joined when everyone has done this. Without letting go of any hands, the group must try to untangle itself.

MUSICAL CHAIRS

GROUP SIZE

10-20. This will not work with a very large group. If your group is larger, you may want to divide them into teams and have one team watch the other play.

GROUP AGE

3-adult

MATERIALS

▶ Roughly enough chairs for everyone to sit—it will not affect the game if you are missing a few.

PURPOSE

Learning to work together as a group

DIRECTIONS

In *Maybe, Maybe Not*, Robert Fulghum offers a unique way to play musical chairs. First, he suggests playing it in the traditional way we all learned as children, but removing several chairs every time the music stops to keep the game moving. After someone has claimed the last chair, discuss how everyone feels about the game.

Next, tell everyone the object of the game will be for *everyone* to find a place to sit down every time the music stops. Remove only a couple of chairs the first time the music stops. People will decide to scramble for laps, etc. Each time remove a few more chairs until everyone is attempting to sit on one chair. Ask the group to consider why this game feels different from the first way it was played. The group will probably discover that including others is always more fun than excluding them. This is an excellent game for a night that deals with church or community.

SANDMAN

GROUP SIZE

10+. The only limit on the size of the group is that everyone must be able to have visual contact with everyone else.

GROUP AGE

Intergenerational

MATERIALS

- None

PURPOSE

Fun

DIRECTIONS

Tell the group the Sandman is coming to put them to sleep. No one knows who the Sandman is, but she will put you to sleep by winking at you. The idea is to catch the Sandman before she catches you. If you look at the Sandman and she winks at you, you must instantly put your head down and keep it there until the game is over. But if you see someone wink at another person and his head goes down, you may accuse the winker of being the Sandman.

Prepare someone in advance to play the Sandman and warn that person not to tell anyone. Explain the directions carefully to the group, showing the children how the Sandman might wink at them. Don't be too concerned if they get "put to sleep" and don't respond. Once somebody guesses the Sandman, the game is over. If you want to have a second round, go around the group and whisper in each person's ear "You are not the Sandman." In one person's ear whisper "You are the Sandman." Play again.

This is a purely-for-fun game, but it can be helpful encouraging children to make eye contact with others.

BUTTON, BUTTON, WHO'S GOT THE BUTTON?

GROUP SIZE

Any size

GROUP AGE

Works best with young children or family groups with many young children

MATERIALS

- A button. In choosing a button, keep in mind the size of the hands of the younger people who will be playing.

PURPOSE

Fun

DIRECTIONS

This is an old birthday party game. Have everyone sit in a circle and hold out both hands, palms pressed together, as if in prayer, fingers pointed straight out. The leader says that he has a button and he will go around the group and give it to someone. You must watch carefully to discover who has the button, but don't say anything until you are asked.

The leader presses his hands together in the same praying manner, only with a button in the palms. He goes around the circle, pushing his hands through each of the outstretched pairs of hands. It is important to demonstrate how to do this to the group, so that young people will keep the bottom of their palms pressed together while the leader's hands are in theirs. The leader tries to make it look as if he is dropping the button into each person's hands. Everyone must be warned to keep their hands pressed tightly together so they will not reveal whether or not they have the button.

The button is eventually dropped into one person's hands and the leader continues on around the group. Then he asks the group to tell him who has the button. Members must raise their hands, palms still pressed together. The first person to guess correctly becomes the "button person" und the game is played again.

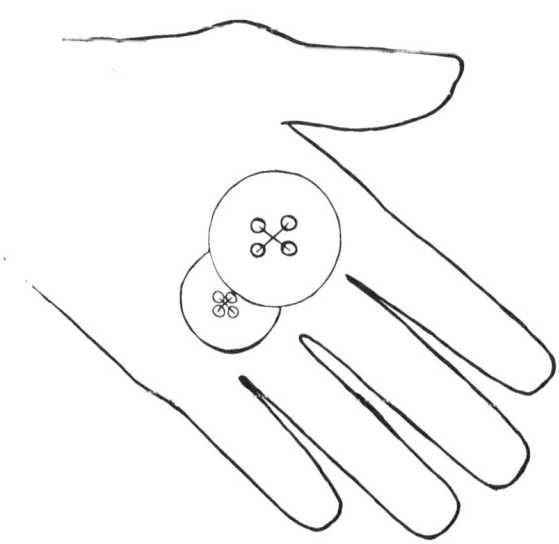

MORE STATUES

GROUP SIZE

Teams of 6 to 10 people

GROUP AGE

Intergenerational

MATERIALS

▶ None

PURPOSE

Working together

DIRECTIONS

Divide the group into subgroups of 6-10 people. If you are working with an intergenerational group, make sure there is a mixture of ages in each group, since this would be too abstract a task for a group of little ones. The leader must choose in advance what the group will be "statueing." Ideas that work well: church, family, school, community, the particular community in which you are doing the exercise.

Each group will be given the same topic, e.g., church. Ask the groups to make a statue (it is allowed to have moving parts) that demonstrates what they think church is or how they feel about it. Give all the groups about 10 minutes to work, then ask them to share their statues with everyone else. Let the rest of the group guess what the parts of the statue mean. If it needs explanation, the statue group can explain, or change the statue to demonstrate better.

NEW LIFE SCAVENGER HUNT

GROUP SIZE

Any size, divided into groups of 6-8

GROUP AGE

Intergenerational, little ones with parents

MATERIALS

- Paper bags for each group
- An open outside space. This is an OUTSIDE, SPRINGTIME game. Note: This game will not work in the city, except in a park.

PURPOSE

Working together

DIRECTIONS

Divide your group into teams of similar size, mixing ages up but keeping small ones with parents for their own safety. Tell the groups they are to go outside and find signs of new life. They do not all have to be traditional signs, like seeds. The group may want to bring something and argue that it is a sign of new life. The group as a whole will decide whether or not the sign is legitimate.

This game takes a little longer than most. Tell the they have 15 minutes, and make sure someone in the group has a watch. They will have one item they have found deducted for every minute they are late. (A penalty is important to prevent people from simply wandering off for the evening!)

Teams return with items they have found and explain why each is a sign of new life. The group as a whole can eliminate any articles they feel are not legitimate signs of life. One item is deducted for every minute a team is late. The team with the largest number of true "signs of new life" wins.

WHO AM I?

GROUP SIZE

Any size

GROUP AGE

Intergenerational

MATERIALS

- Straight pins
- Slips of paper with the name of a biblical character written on each, enough so that each person in the group will have one, sample characters given below

PURPOSE

Working together

Sample list of characters:

Adam	Eve	Cain	Abel
Noah	Abraham	Isaac	Jacob
Esau	Leah	Rachel	Rebecca
Joseph	Judah	Benjamin	Saul
David	Solomon	Isaiah	Jeremiah
Ruth	Deborah	Samson	Mary
Jesus	Elizabeth	Joseph	Simon
John the Baptist		Andrew	Peter
James	John	Paul	Matthew
Herod	Pilate	Anna	Nicodemus
Judas			

DIRECTIONS

Write the name of a biblical character on each slip of paper, focusing on characters that have been part of the learning experience this year. As members enter, a name is pinned on their backs. The names of easy characters, such as Mary, Joseph, Jesus, Adam, Eve, Noah, and Abraham should be saved for the young children, while adults are given the most difficult names.

Once everyone has arrived, explain to the group that they must discover who they are. They are allowed to ask each person in the community one question that can be answered in one word, e.g., "What kind of job did I have?" "Fisherman." When they think they know who they are, members can go sit down. Young children are not bound by the one-word-answer rule and should be given big hints: e.g., "You were killed by your brother, Cain." When everyone (or almost everyone) is seated, ask each person who he thinks he is and why. Then have each stand up and turn around. If they are right, applaud and take the slip of paper off. If they are not right, someone in the group should help them out, e.g., "You are right thinking you are Peter because he was a fisherman, but this fisherman never became the head of the Church, even though he met Jesus before his brother, Peter." Hints should be broad and easy, at this point. As soon as someone guesses who she is, everyone should applaud. If there are people who have not yet guessed who they are, they should stand with their backs to the group while people give them hints. Explain to the group that some of the characters are far more difficult and lesser known than others, if they don't see this readily. As people guess who they are, have them sit down.

This game takes a little longer than the other icebreakers but it can be an excellent review for a group that has been studying Scripture.

BIBLICAL TIME LINE

GROUP SIZE

Any size

GROUP AGE

Intergenerational

MATERIALS

- Index cards with a historical biblical character on each
- Bibles

PURPOSE

Review

DIRECTIONS

On entering the home or group, each person is given a card with a name on it. When everyone is present, ask the group to arrange themselves in chronological order, beginning with Adam and Eve. Bibles can be used, and people are free to ask one another for help. Easy characters should be given to younger children.

This can be a great way to get people in line for a potluck supper, or any social event that requires taking turns. It also provides a way to review Bible characters and their place in history.

CIRCLE GAMES

BACKGROUND

If the majority of children in your group are preschoolers, old-fashioned circle games are wonderful icebreakers and can be used throughout a gathering. Young children have much shorter attention spans, and it does not hurt a lesson to break for 10 minutes in the middle for a game.

DIRECTIONS

In selecting games, be careful about using ones such as *Farmer in the Dell*, where an arbitrary selection process lakes place and some children may be left out. Games that work well: *a Tisket, a Tasket, Little Sally Saucer, Bluebird, Butcher Shop, London Bridge*, or any that give everyone an equal opportunity to join in. Local libraries should have copies of words and music for most of these games. Circle games have existed for over 2,000 years. We should not underestimate their importance in the development of a child or a community.

SIMON SAYS

BACKGROUND

Simon Says is another one of those games that can be pulled out when your mind is blank and you have no icebreaker for the evening. Doing the *Hokey Pokey* is fun with a group that is not too inhibited. Check out some of the games from your childhood, from Scouts and 4-H and other group activities. You'll find many that can be modified for community and classroom.

PART 2
SOCIAL & SERVICE IDEAS

The ideas expressed in this part of the book are simply meant to jump-start your own brainstorming ideas for social and service activities for families. They are tentatively placed according to season, but many would work at different times of the year, particularly in different climates. These are an aid to your ingenuity, not a replacement for it.

AUTUMN SOCIAL ACTIVITIES

APPLE PICKING

If you live in the northern regions, fall is a wonderful time for picking apples as a group. Families can pick apples for themselves, for a charity or soup kitchen, or make pies for a bake sale to raise money for a charitable endeavor. Most children appreciate the opportunity. Many orchards offer hayrides along with apple picking.

If your church has a large hall or gathering space, come together after picking apples to play games like dunking for apples or trying to get a bite out of an apple dangled on a string. While one group is playing, another can be making apple crunch or apple pie to be served with cider.

LEAF WAXING

This is another activity that is limited to those areas that actually experience autumn with changing foliage. Arrange a fall picnic for the families. We have found it is easiest to organize by using the potluck format. Plan the picnic for a wooded park, and have the families take a walk before the meal and search for beautiful leaves. Ask everyone to choose a favorite leaf, one that represents him or her in some way. They are to bring these leaves back and explain to other family members why they were chosen.

Wax the leaves by melting household wax in large cans placed on grills. Dip the leaves in the wax, and place them on waxed paper to dry. Leaves waxed in this way will last about a month and serve as a happy reminder of an enjoyable autumn day.

HALLOWEEN

Trunk-or-treating: At Mount Saint Virgin School in New Jersey, families celebrate trunk-or-treating. Families decorate the trunks of their cars or pickup trucks for Halloween and park in the school parking lot. Some go to great lengths to simulate graveyards and haunted houses in trucks and vans. Children come in costume and trick or treat from car to car, then join in a party in the school gym. Many parents come in costume as well, and it is a great opportunity for families to play with one another as well as with the other members of their community.

Pumpkin Carving: Gather families together for a pumpkin carving contest. Each family brings their own pumpkin, candle, and cutting utensils. The parish supplies covered areas for the task of carving, choosing the winners, and refreshments.

Prizes can be offered for the scariest, the funniest, the overall best, the most original. Prizes should be something that can be shared by the whole family, such as certificates for pizza.

Haunted Houses: Children love making haunted houses as much as they like going through them. Invite families who are interested to come to set it up and the rest of the parish to visit. Tapes are available with scary haunted house sounds, fake cobwebs can be bought in stores, and rubber bugs and gushy noodles can be scary in the dark. Children will have lots of creative ideas. The objective is not to create a spectacular haunted house, but to have fun doing it.

THANKSGIVING DINNER

If you do not have family with whom to share your dinner, plan dinner some place where several families in a similar situation can share the meal. This could be a church hall, if you have one large enough and comfortable enough.

THANKSGIVING LEFTOVERS

Plan a potluck supper for the Thanksgiving weekend. The only stipulation is that everyone must bring leftovers.

AUTUMN SERVICE ACTIVITIES

BACK TO SCHOOL CLOTHING DRIVE

Fall is the perfect time for a clothing drive. Most families are sorting through school clothes for the year to discover what is needed and what has been outgrown. Have children launder and fold clothes to be donated as their part of the gift. Set up tables marked with different clothing sizes in a gathering space at the church. Once all the families have found the appropriate spots for their clothes, the clothes can be boxed and transported. Clothes carefully prepared are far more usable to the St. Vincent de Paul Society or Goodwill, and children learn the value of sharing them as a gift, rather than discarding them in a heap.

Once everything is ready for shipment, celebrate with a snack.

WELCOME THE STRANGER

The beginning of the school year is particularly difficult for new children in a school. Ask everyone in your program to make a special effort to welcome someone new, inviting that person to join at least one activity with their established group of friends. This is a far more difficult task for the teen and preteen than it may appear to parents or to younger siblings, but this is a critical time for teaching them to reach out to others.

YARD WORK

If there are elders in your community who need help raking leaves, putting up storm windows, and generally preparing for winter, set aside a day to do the work and organize work teams of families to get it done.

SHARE THE BOUNTY

Judith Dunlap of Dayton, Ohio, initiated this Halloween activity. On the Sunday before Halloween, she invited parishioners to submit the names and addresses of children away at college. The children in the parish were invited to bring some of their candy to the church hall on the Saturday following Halloween. Together, they packaged the candy and wrote notes to all the college students. The college students appreciate being remembered, and it helps to keep them connected with the parish.

Saint Catherine of Siena Parish in Menden, New York, takes it a step further and bakes cookies several times a year to send to its college students. This could be done by gathering together to do the baking and the shipping, or having the baking donated and the families gathered to do the packing and shipping.

JUNK IN A TRUNK

Raise money for a family in need or a charity in the community by having a yard sale out of car trunks. Everyone labels and brings their own items for sale in the trunks of their cars. In the church parking lot, or other large gathering space, the cars are parked and trunks are opened. Each family is responsible for selling their own junk and taking home anything that isn't sold. All proceeds are donated. Advertise the event well in local papers and church bulletins of neighboring parishes, letting everyone know what the money is for.

CAKE-LESS CAKE SALE

This is another way of raising money for an immediate need or a local charity. This is a fundraiser for busy people. Invite your families to make their own cakes, decide how much they are worth, send in the money, and eat the cake. The recipes can also be donated and then sold for a dollar.

COMMUNITY FUNDRAISERS

Invite your families to participate as a group in one of the many community walkathons and bikeathons that are sponsored in the fall and the spring. Choose causes that have particular appeal to your group of families: research for a disease someone in your group has, such as the MS walkathon, Easter Seals walk if you have someone with birth defects, etc.

THANKSGIVING DINNER

Celebrate Thanksgiving by serving in a soup kitchen.

FOOD BASKETS

Many agencies prepare food baskets and ask for donations of nonperishable foods. It is much more fun for children to see what actually happens in that preparation. Find out what your local agencies put in their food baskets. Collect the food, and on the weekend before Thanksgiving, gather as a large group and make up the baskets yourselves. Donate them fully assembled. You may even consider a fundraiser to provide turkeys for the baskets.

ADVENT & CHRISTMAS SOCIAL ACTIVITIES

"NEW YEAR'S" PARTY

Advent is the beginning of the Church year. Many are more familiar with the Jewish new year, *Rosh Hashanna*, than we are with our own, probably because we do not celebrate ours.

Plan a family New Year's Eve Party for Saturday evening before the first Sunday of Advent. You will want this to be a real party with good food and music to make an impression. Ask people to come as "tables": a gathering of families that are friends to sit together for the party. Make sure there are noisemakers, bubbles, and New Year's Eve type favors at each table. Explain to your families that the new year actually begins with Vespers this evening. Say a simple Vespers prayer as your opening (the Magnificat would be appropriate), then wish everyone "Happy New Year." The group can respond with noisemakers and greeting everyone. Then it is time to party.

CAROLING

Christmas caroling is a wonderful way to remind people of the true meaning of Christmas. Many convalescent homes welcome carolers at Christmas time, but be aware that some are inundated. You may want to simply do this in a neighborhood where you know most of the people. You could end at the home of one of your families with hot chocolate.

You can also carol in a large group at the church and invite people to come and listen and join in. The point is not to sing well. The point is to sing songs everyone knows and wants to sing.

This is far more fun when it is done outside. If you don't have a grotto or special statue where you can gather, simply use the steps of the church. End with refreshments and hot chocolate in the hall. Keep the evening simple and under an hour. It will become a tradition in the parish very quickly.

COOKIE SWAP

Cookie swaps are today's busy family's response to the multitude of cookies our grandmothers made at Christmas. Every family bakes two to four dozen cookies of one recipe. (You may need to suggest that it not be chocolate chip, since you may wind up with all chocolate chip cookies.) The cookies are arranged on platters and brought to the swap. Each family also brings a box for the cookies they will take home.

Cookie trays are lined up on tables and families walk by them, picking and choosing the same number of cookies they brought to the swap and taking home a box of assorted cookies.

This can become a service activity simply by using half the cookies to make plates for the shut-ins in the community and arranging visits.

ADVENT & CHRISTMAS SERVICE ACTIVITIES

CHRISTMAS GIVING

1. Check with social services in your area, and see if there are families that will not be celebrating Christmas. Pair your parish families with these families, and have them prepare Christmas gifts. It is important *not* to be extravagant in this gift giving. The meaning of Christmas is not the gifts, but it is difficult for young children to receive no gifts when so many of their peers will be inundated with new toys.

2. Check with groups that sponsor toy collections for needy children. Encourage families to set aside some of their own Christmas money to buy a toy for one of these collections or to raise the money through some family or group activity. Baking Christmas cookies and having a cookie sale can provide money for toys and Christmas dinners.

CHRISTMAS CARDS

Inquire about the elderly and lonely in the parish who may not be hearing from many people at Christmas. Have the children make cards to send. These can be colored or painted or made from last year's cards.

ADVENT LETTERS

The reason we send cards and give gifts to one another on Jesus' birthday is simply that we are recognizing the Jesus incarnate in all of us. Instead of just sending cards this year, write notes to people who may not expect them, or who have been "Jesus" to you in some way during the year. Thank them.

FOOD BANKS

Poor people need food every day, not just on holidays. This is an excellent time to plan a regular monthly food collection for the food bank in your area. Ask children to collect and return bottles and donate the change for purchasing fresh foods.

NURSING HOMES

Make group visits to nursing homes in the area. This is a very lonely time of year for many of the inhabitants. Even though many homes get inundated with visitors at this time of year, there are still many people within them who are lonely and would benefit from having an individual or family come and sit with them. Nursing homes will be happy to point out which clients could use visitors. Families can go to visit individuals and meet back at the church to pray for them or just celebrate with refreshments.

HOLY FAMILY SUNDAY

HOLY FAMILY LITURGY AND CALENDAR BLESSING

The feast of the Holy Family falls on the Sunday between Christmas and New Year's Day, and is the perfect time for a celebration of family life. Ask the pastor to allow entire families to serve as ushers and greeters, as readers and servers at the liturgy. Children who already serve can teach their parents, even if their parents have never had the experience.

Some mothers who were denied the opportunity to be servers as children may welcome the chance. Have families take up the collection and lead the singing. Choose Christmas carols for the music that are easy and well known.

Invite all your households and all other parishioners to bring their calendars for the new year to the liturgy. At the presentation of the gifts, have one member in each family bring the calendar forward and place it in front of the altar.

The homily should focus on making time to listen to God and to listen as God speaks through our family. The sacredness of all time needs to be stressed. Since this is a family liturgy with an emphasis on children, it may be possible within your diocesan regulations to have a parent or a couple speak in place of the homily. After Communion, the celebrant blesses the calendars:

"Loving God, you are the beginning and the end, the Alpha and the Omega. Help us to remember that time is your gift. The only time we truly have is the present. Keep us present to you and to one another in your eternal NOW, and bless all our efforts to do so… *(celebrant sprinkles calendars with holy water)*… you, who are Father, Son, and Holy Spirit to us. Amen."

Continue with the liturgy.

Have refreshments after the liturgy.

HOLY FAMILY PARTY

Holy Family Sunday is a good time for a Christmas party. The preholiday rush is past and families are more relaxed, more willing to take time to be together. Serve cupcakes and hide bean seeds in three of them. The people who find the seeds get to be the three kings for the entrance procession for the feast of Epiphany.

WINTER & LENTEN SOCIAL ACTIVITIES

LITURGICAL TABLECLOTHS

This can also be used as an Advent or Easter activity.

Invite families to come to a "tablecloth party" and to bring a piece of "Indianhead" cotton large enough—and of the appropriate color for cloth—for their usual meal table, and smocks or old shirts to cover themselves. Provide stencils of lenten (Advent/Easter) symbols cut out of water-resistant paper, such as meat-packing paper. Parish clip art books are a good source of symbols.

Work areas will need to be thoroughly covered. Each work area will need large brushes, extra paper, waterproof paint, scissors, and common pins. Families are invited to choose from the provided stencils or to make their own. The stencils are pinned to the material. The symbol is painted by brushing paint across the edges of the paper toward the center of the symbol (so as not to force paint under the outside edges of the symbol). A symbol can be used several times on one cloth, or several different symbols can be used. Families are invited to take the cloths home and use them throughout the liturgical season.

Symbols can also be cut out of iron-on patches and ironed on to the cloth, or cut out of felt and stuck on with fabric tape. Waterproof paint washes best of all these choices, but is the messiest to work with.

SKATING PARTIES

Winter can be a good time for gathering families for skating parties, whether roller or ice. Many roller rinks will rent out the entire rink for an evening, allow you to choose your own music, and, in some cases, bring in your own food. If you have no large gathering place at your church, this can offer a happy alternative for a potluck supper.

Outdoor parties work best in areas where it is legal to have a campfire, for warmth and marshmallows, and where there are some hills for sledding for those who don't skate.

MARDI GRAS PARTY

Mardi Gras is the Tuesday before Ash Wednesday and the last celebration before the beginning of Lent. Plan a potluck supper, and have party hats and noisemakers. Prepare a large box covered with purple paper, with a foil cross on top and a large sign with an "Alleluia" on it.

Celebrate your supper. End with some crazy songs, a clown doing tricks, a talent show, etc. At the closing, have everyone cheer loudly and blow their noisemakers. If you have decorated with balloons, have everyone pop balloons at the same moment. Then ask everyone to be very quiet. (It helps to lower the lights.) Take down the "Alleluia," and place it in the box. Invite everyone to walk forward quietly and place their noisemakers in the box. Put the lid on the box, and keep it in a prominent place until Easter.

On Easter morning, have some children carry the "Alleluia" sign in the entrance procession.

PANCAKE TUESDAY

Mardi Gras is also known as "Pancake Tuesday." Pancake Tuesday is English in origin. On the night before Lent began, pancakes were made to use up the butter and fat before the community began its fast.

Gather your families for a pancake supper. Assign different tasks to different families: setup, cleanup, shopping, cooking, serving, entertaining.

SAINT PATRICK'S DAY

March is a long month and Saint Patrick's Day can offer a break in the somber lenten atmosphere. Invite families to a simple potluck supper, but everyone must wear something green and bring something green to eat. Give everyone name tags, but begin all last names with an O' or Mc.

Prepare a storyteller to tell the tale of Saint Patrick. Invite everyone who would like to perform to prepare a poem to recite or a ballad to sing, in the tradition of the Irish come-all-ye. If you have any Irish step dancers, invite them to perform and to teach the group.

ETHNIC PARTIES

Patron saints of other strong ethnic groups can be celebrated with similar parties and traditions. Be sensitive to the nationalities and customs that are strong in your area and celebrate the saint days.

WINTER & LENTEN SERVICE ACTIVITIES

VALENTINE'S DAY

1. Plan a Valentine's party for a local convalescent home. One or more families can be responsible for each aspect: food, games, cards for each of the people, music, etc. Invite families together on a weekend afternoon before Valentine's Day to plan. Check with the local home you hope to visit for what is allowed and what might be too stressful for the visitors.

2. Plan a party for a school in an underprivileged area. It may simply involve making cupcakes with hearts for all the classes and small packets of candy for each of the children.

3. Make valentine cards for shut-ins in the parish. Hand deliver them on Valentine's Day with small baskets of candies or cupcakes with hearts. Even if the homebound can't eat the goodies, they will appreciate receiving them. Most parishes have a list of those housebound members who would appreciate a visit. While you are visiting, check to see if there is anything to be done that someone in the group could help out with.

BOOK COLLECTION

Most prisons are constantly searching for books for inmates. If you do not know any prisons in your area, check with your state representative. Collect books, clean, and sort into categories, pack and ship.

SHELTERS

In cities, shelters are in need of extra help throughout the winter. Depending on the size of your program, you could offer to help a shelter all winter, with families take turns fulfilling the obligation. Most of the help needed is in feeding, distributing blankets, and cleaning up.

SOUP KITCHENS

Like the shelters, winter is a difficult time for the soup kitchens. Investigate to see if any in your area need help. Many ask groups to take one day a week, or one day a month, when they will be responsible for making sandwiches. This is an excellent way to involve young children since it is something they can actually do. The group gathers at the church hall or some other designated area to make the sandwiches. Everyone is responsible for bringing something. When the sandwiches are made, they are delivered by one or two people to the soup kitchen.

SNOW REMOVAL

If you live in an area where there is snow in winter, find out which people in your neighborhood and parish could use help with snow removal. Set up a schedule so that there will always be a family prepared to help when it snows.

ASSISTING THE ELDERLY

While the elderly deserve our special attention all year long, winter can be an especially difficult time for them to get out in areas where the weather gets cold. Set up a shopping committee to make sure they are getting the supplies they need. Instruct people buying groceries to deliver them in person, to make sure the house is warm enough when they arrive and that the homeowners have fuel.

PASSION SUNDAY

Search out someone in your parish who is adept at making things from palms. Invite them to meet with families after one of the Masses on Passion Sunday to make objects like crosses and crowns of thorns from the palms. Visit the elderly shut-ins of the parish, or people in convalescent homes, and offer the palms as gifts. Many will have made similar things when they were young and will enjoy receiving them.

HOLY WEEK LITURGY PLANNING AND PARTICIPATION

Involve different groups in your parish to take on the responsibility for planning the different liturgies of Holy Week. For example, the faith formation families could be involved in the planning of Passion Sunday. Encourage families to participate fully in all the liturgies, bringing bells to ring on Holy Thursday and Holy Saturday, their own branches on Passion Sunday, and having their feet washed on Holy Thursday. If they buried an "Alleluia" at a Mardi Gras party, the children should bring that in the entrance procession on Easter morning.

EASTER SEASON SOCIAL ACTIVITIES

PLANTERS

Invite your families to come together to make planters. You will need to know the number of families involved to be able to provide materials. Investigate the cost of the materials and charge families accordingly.

Seek out a carpenter in your community and have him/her cut the wood pieces of the planters to size. An Easter symbol can be carved into the front with a jigsaw before the planters are painted or stained, or the symbol could be painted on afterward. Buy enough potting soil for all the planters, and invite the families to bring the paint or stain that will match their homes and the plants, bulbs, or seeds they want to put in the planters. They will also need hammers and nails; caution them to come in old clothes.

The pieces for each planter are placed in separate piles in an outdoor area. If symbols have not been carved on the boxes, make small templates of Easter symbols and have extra paint available. Invite the families to assemble, fill, and plant.

You may want to end with a blessing for the new life and the planters. Ask everyone to put their planters where they can be seen easily from the road, so as other families drive or walk by, they will see the sign of another member of their community.

WIND CHIMES

Many craft stores sell kits for wind chimes. Painting them and putting them together is a particularly appropriate activity for a Pentecost party. The Spirit is the wind that brings out the music in all of us. Gather your families to put the chimes together. You may want to put gifts and fruits of the Spirit on the chimes themselves. End with a simple prayer service on the Spirit, such as "Holy Spirit Prayer" on page 137.

POTLUCK PICNIC

Plan a potluck picnic for your families in a local park with plenty of space for the children to play. Assign parts of the meal to names beginning with certain letters of the alphabet, e.g., A through D bring salads, etc. You may not wind up with everything you need, but that is part of the fun.

POTLUCK SCRIPTURE

Plan a potluck picnic, as above. Every family coming to the picnic gets the name of a biblical character and some Scripture references about them. They must learn something about that person (when they lived, etc.) before coming to the picnic. Stick to the historical books in choosing characters, since that will make it easier.

When everyone gets to the picnic and the food is put out, they must form a timeline to get in line for food. Adam and Eve would come first, followed by Cain, then Abel, etc.

Wait until everyone is lined up before serving the food. If someone gets stuck, help them out a little or have them ask one another for help.

"OLIMPING" GAMES

Create a series of silly races, e.g., a three-legged race run backwards, breaking balloons your team has tied all over you, carrying water in a sieve, water balloon tosses. The idea is to make funny situations that allow family members to laugh at themselves, not to compete seriously. People can be organized into teams, play as families, or play as family groups. "Roni's"—a large macaroni shell mounted on an upside down paper cup, all painted silver—are awarded for the best in every activity. Making up the races and creating the "roni's" are the only tasks involved.

Invite everyone in the group to bring refreshments to be shared.

PILGRIMAGE

If you have an outdoor shrine in your area, plan a pilgrimage. Plan a picnic as part of the activity.

If you have recently completed a unit on the Hebrew Scriptures (Old Testament), plan your "pilgrimage" to a synagogue and ask the local rabbi to talk to the group about his or her community's symbols and traditions.

After covering the Sermon on the Mount, plan your pilgrimage to a large, open hill that will not be too difficult for the little ones to climb up. Have different people prepare to tell different parts of the Sermon on the Mount in contemporary language.

PENTECOST PARTY

Pentecost is the birthday of the Church. Make a birthday cake for the liturgy and invite everyone to join in singing "Happy Birthday" and eating the cake after Mass. Since it is usually warm in most areas by Pentecost, an outside liturgy and picnic could be planned. This can be a good way to bring the year to a close.

Any of the activities or prayer services on the Holy Spirit could be used as part of a Pentecost party.

OUTDOOR EUCHARIST

An outdoor Mass followed by a picnic is a great way to bring the year to a close and to celebrate Pentecost.

EASTER SEASON SERVICE ACTIVITIES

LITTER HIKE

Plan a litter hike around community Earth Day activities. Have families sign up in advance, and appoint captains for neighborhood teams. Put the names of captains, their areas, starting places and times, on lists at the back of church, and have families sign up for different teams. All teams meet at the church at a specified time for refreshments. Money from any bottle—or aluminum can—returns is donated to a local charity.

PLAYGROUND CLEANUP

If there are no playgrounds in your area that need cleaning up, arrange a day that families from the parish can go into a nearby city and volunteer with a group cleaning up a park in that area, Many parent groups are getting grants for playground equipment that has to be assembled by parents. Watch the paper for announcements of city groups looking for support in building playgrounds, and join in.

YARD ASSISTANCE

Invite families to sign up for a "yard day." People in the parish who find it difficult to keep up their yards—rake, plant flowers, etc.—can sign up for spring assistance. It is the leader's job to check out the various homes, talk with owners about what needs to be done, and assign families for the day. A spaghetti supper or cookout at church following the effort offers support and thanks to those who have worked all day. Invite those who needed the help to join in the meal with the workers.

HABITAT FOR HUMANITY

Habitat for Humanity exists in most of our cities. Invite families to join in a work force for habitat construction. Children as young as six can be great helpers as "gofers."

GARAGE/TAG SALES

Garage sales are an excellent way to raise money for a charity or a family in need. Garage sale shoppers like to go from one sale to another, so plan them close together. This is an excellent opportunity for all of us to simplify and dispose of what we no longer use or need. Check out the autumn service activities for the "junk in a trunk" sale.

RENEWING THE EARTH

If there is a neglected area in your town, a park that could use sprucing up, a main street that could use some flowers, check with your town about the possibility of families forming a beautification committee and working together to clean the area and plant shrubs and flowers.

CHURCH BEAUTIFICATION

Gather families to clean the church for the spring, and to assist with grounds work. This type of activity gives young people a strong sense of ownership.

SUMMER SOCIAL AND SERVICE ACTIVITIES

CAMPING

A family campout weekend is a great experience for families who have already developed some sense of belonging to the larger community.

FAMILY DRIVE-IN

Rent videos of good family films, and show them outside on the church lawn. Invite people to bring picnic suppers. If your parish is in the city, see if it is possible to meet in a park. You will need battery or generator-operated equipment, but you might attract other interested people to your community.

FAMILY PET SHOWS

Have a pet show for family pets. Offer prizes for the most friendly, the most unusual, the cleanest, etc. Keep the reasons for winning simple, things that families will enjoy. As a subcategory to a pet show, you may want to have a frisbee catching contest for dogs, or a frog jumping contest.

FAMILY RETREAT WEEKS

For those parishes that cannot offer a family program during the year, family retreat weeks are an excellent alternative. It is essential, though, that families go *away* for this type of weekend. There are too many distractions at home. Many of the "Family Day Activities" given in this book could be combined to create a retreat experience. Many of the topical whole family resources from The Pastoral Center can be modified into family retreats.

FUNDRAISERS

Summer time, with its less hectic schedule, can be a good time for raising money to cover medical expenses for a local family, support the local soup kitchen, or donate to some other worthwhile charity.

- Bikeathons—Have short distances for young children in safe areas, such as the church parking lot, and longer distances for others
- Walkathons—Encourage families to use strollers and wagons so that all can participate
- Car washes—Have families sign up for times they will help

PART 3
FAMILY DAY EVENTS

These events are designed for gathering groups of families together for an activity that ts both fun and educational. They all have a spiritual component. They can be used individually as family days in the parish, or grouped together for family retreats. Prayer services from the fourth section of this book can easily be added to any of the experiences, to give them a stronger spiritual focus and an element of ritual.

SAINTS ALIVE

OVERVIEW

The following activity forms an excellent opening for a religious education program, whether in family or classroom. It can also be used as an All Saints Day celebration, a Holy Family Sunday celebration, or a closing activity at the end of the religious education year.

This is the only activity given in this book where parents and children are separated, since the primary aim of this text is to enable parents and children to share faith. However, I have found that taking time to directly offer parents encouragement, affirmation, and support helps them to enter into the year and any other activities that are planned with far more confidence. The activity is simply designed to emphasize the sacred role of parenting and affirm the parent's ability to fulfill the role of primary educator.

MATERIALS

- Colored sheets of cellophane
- Lightweight cardboard or heavy paper (white)
- Glue
- String
- Staplers
- Old magazines
- Scissors
- Index cards
- Translation of Colossians 3:12-15 from the "old" Jerusalem Bible
- *Holiness Family Style* video and player (optional: see the adult experience section for more information)

REMOTE PREPARATION

1. Prepare your talking points for the adult experience or watch the video yourself so that you will be prepared for what the parents are going to learn and will want to discuss.

2. Prepare several people to work with the children. Older teens work well in this role, and young adults, single or married, are wonderful. If you need to use parents, share the video with them first, so that they will not miss this part of the experience.

3. Cut out the outline for "stained glass windows," using a razor or an X-Acto™ knife.

4. Leave a large solid circle in the middle. (See a sample template on the next page.) You will need one for every child.

5. Prepare a large work space for the children in proximity to the area where the parents will be meeting. Plan work areas for six to eight children, with window templates and twelve inch pieces of string for each child, pieces of colored cellophane, magic markers, glue, scissors, and magazines.

6. Read the passage from Colossians as part of your prayer during the week preceding the gathering.

ADULT EXPERIENCE

1. As families enter, give each parent an index card. Ask them to write their "preferred" name on it. It can be their baptismal name, nickname, or whichever name they prefer.

2. Begin by singing "Holy Ground."

3. Take a moment to welcome everyone. Ask parents to give their name cards to their children, then ask the children to introduce their parents to the parents around them.

4. Invite the children to take the cards with them, and to leave. Leaders prepared to work with them will take them to their work space.

5. Take a few moments to introduce yourself to the parents, and then speak a moment about why they are gathering separately today. If you will be showing the video, don't overdo the introduction since there is a lot of talking on the video. Just let them know you want them to understand their holiness

6. Present the content, either by following the siggested talking points or showing them the video. Read the next sections for more information on these options.

7. Allow time at the end for quiet and a few moments for people to talk to one another before the children return. This discussion works better if you do not set up formal questions. People will want to react and interact.

OPTION 1: HOLINESS FAMILY STYLE VIDEO

This 30 minute video was filmed in 2008, so it may look a bit dated, but it is engaging and the key points remain relevant.

The video is available to stream online for free, or you can purchase a DVD from The Pastoral Center for a nominal cost. For information on either, see http://pastoral.center/holiness-family-style.

OPTION 2: TALKING POINTS

Alternately, you can use the talking points in the next section to present on this topic of holiness in family life. Rather than reading the points word-for-word to your attendees, use them to prepare beforehand and make the talk your own. Your presentation will benefit from any examples you can add from your own experiences of family life.

The talking points are roughly based on the content in the video. If possible, watch the video as part of your preparation.

ADULT EXPERIENCE TALKING POINTS

Where Holiness Happens

▶ Many of us who have been raised Catholic may have gotten the impression that all of the important and holy things happen inside the church building. Where did we ever get such a strange idea? Not from Jesus!

▶ Where did Jesus do his first miracle? (At Cana.) And what was happening there? (A wedding.) And what did he do? He changed water into wine for a family party. Did you ever wonder what all that water was doing there? It was water for ritual purification. It was holy water, and Jesus turned it into wine so we would forever remember that no ritual was more important than the love that was celebrated here. And we forgot it immediately.

Who Is Holy?

▶ Maybe one of the ways we went wrong was in misinterpreting something Jesus said. Do you remember the story of the Rich Young Man, who asked, "Master, what must I do to be saved?" And Jesus said, "Keep the commandments." And he replied, "But I've done that since I was very young." And Jesus said, "If you would be perfect, go, sell what you have, give to the poor, and come, follow me."

▶ Who are the people in the church we think of today who sold what they had, gave to the poor, and followed the Lord? The priests, nuns, and brothers. The religious and professional holy people.

▶ All of us who get married and/or start families may think of ourselves as not quite good and not quite holy.

▶ But that's just not true. We, too, sold what we had and gave it away. Many gave up little bank accounts for great big mortgages to house families. Some gave up racy sports cars for clunky minivans.

▶ All of us gave up independence of being single for a new kind of obedience. It is possible to hear the call and follow the Lord as married people. There is only one call for Christian people: baptism.

▶ In March 2018, Pope Francis wrote a letter to all of us on the call to holiness. In it, he says, "To be holy does not require being a bishop, a priest or a religious. We are frequently tempted to think that holiness is only for those who can withdraw from ordinary affairs to spend much time in prayer. That is not the case. We are all called to be holy by living our lives with love and by bearing witness in everything we do, wherever we find ourselves....Are you married? Be holy by loving and caring for your husband or wife, as Christ does for the Church. Do you work for a living? Be holy by labouring with integrity and skill in the service of your brothers and sisters. Are you a parent or grandparent? Be holy by patiently teaching the little ones how to follow Jesus. Are you in a position of authority? Be holy by working for the common good and renouncing personal gain."[3]

When Are We Holy

▶ But there's still that temptation to think of the "professional holy people" and the holy things they do.

▶ Think of the Divine Office, which the Church put together to name the sacred hours of the day: 2am, 6am, 10am, 2pm, 6pm, and 10pm. Monks, sisters, and others stop whatever they are doing (including sleeping) at these times to pray together.

▶ Are these times familiar to any of you? These are feeding times for babies! Who had it first? But the Church decided that moms and dads shouldn't be

---

3 *Gaudete et Exsultate (Rejoice and Be Glad)*, apostolic exhortation, 14.

the only ones up at night, so we get the monks and nuns up with them.

- We are all about the same thing... nourishing the future of the earth. The only difference is, some do it with psalms, some do it with milk.

Experiences of Family Holiness

- The life story of St. Thérèse of Lisieux includes a story in which her Mother Superior asked her to clean dirt out of the cupboards, and put it in a box. Afterwards, the superior spread it in cupboards and told her to do it again.

- That story may make no sense to us until we have parented a toddler and spent long days having our child undo half of what we have done. Thérèse didn't have a toddler, so she needed help to learn the virtue of patience.

- Why did we as lay people lose our sense of holiness? Sacred books wound up being written by monks and nuns, using churchy language. Why? They were the only ones who had time. We lost our holy language.

- In the spiritual classic *The Dark Night of the Soul*, St. John of the Cross explains how you don't get to the heights of holiness until you hit bottom with the absense of all spiritual consolation. For a mom or dad, this is when you sit up all night at the bedside of a four-year-old with fever that won't break. Or when you wait for every paycheck expecting to be laid off or downsized. When teenager has the car for very first time and is 2½ hours late. Spirituality just never got explained in our own language.

Reclaiming Holiness in Family Life

- To be holy is to be like God. God is not a church. God is a family. That's why we say "Father, Son and Holy Spirit." As a family that mirrors God, what is our special ministry? To make God visible. We put skin on God so God can be touched, seen, and known.

- Anyone who ever picked up a crying baby teaches that when you cry out, someone answers. That is central to our undestanding of prayer. Every parent has taught that.

- Or consider playing peek-a-boo with six-month-olds. They are totally startled when we show ourselves again. Just because you can't see me doesn't mean I'm not there. What does that say about God? We teach that.

- We get our little ones ready for school, buying supplies, bathing them, packing snacks. Just like God, who goes before us and prepares the way.

- The Church put a religious name on these things, that have already been taught by parents.

Passing on the Faith

- And then we reach the teenage years and wonder, did they get it? Can they make it their own?

- There is a saying that goes: "There are only two lasting bequests we can give our children. One is roots and the other is wings." We do our best to root our children in the image of God, with rituals that celebrate a sense of the holy and sacred in our ordinary lives. Then it's time to let them go and find their own reasons for belief.

- But so much of own self image is tied up in who our children are and what they become. "Where did I fail? What did I do wrong?"

- Forgiving our children is easy. Forgiving ourselves for their mistakes can be much harder. But, as Mother Teresa said, God doesn't ask me to be successful. God only asks me to be faithful.

- If there is nothing you would want to change about how you have parented, you are either extremely fortunate, very young, or deluded.

- We are not good parents if our children turn out well. We are good parents if *we* turn out well through the process of parenting. What our children become is their choice. One of greatest gifts we can give is the freedom to make that choice.

Matthew 25 Reflection

- I have a vision of all the parents gathered before God on judgment day. The Lord will say to us: "I was hungry and you fed me, thirsty, and you gave me a drink, naked and you clothed me, homeless and you sheltered me, imprisoned and you visited me…"

- And we will interrupt, protesting, "Not, I, Lord. When did I see you hungry and feed you?" And the Lord will say: "How could you ask, you of the three-and-a-half-million peanut butter and jelly sandwiches!"

- "But thirsty, Lord?" "I was in the lemonade line that came in with the summer heat and the flies, and left fingerprints on your walls and mud on your floors, and you gave me a drink."

- "But naked, Lord, homeless?" "I was born to you naked and homeless and you sheltered me, first in wombs and then in arms. You clothed me with your love, and spent the next twenty years keeping me in jeans."

- "But imprisoned, Lord? I know I didn't see you in prison. I've never even been in a prison." "Oh, yes. For I was imprisoned in my littleness behind the bars of a crib and I cried out in the night, and you came. I was imprisoned inside a twelve-year-old body that was exploding with many new emotions, I didn't know who I was any more, and you loved me into being myself. And I was imprisoned behind my teenage anger, my rebellion, and my headphones, and you waited outside my locked door for me to let you in.

- "Now, Beloved, enter into the joy which has been prepared for you for all eternity."

- Amen.

CHILDREN EXPERIENCE

The explanation for the children can be given by one leader, but several will be needed to help the children with the task of making the windows.

1. Ask the children to sit with their siblings. Friends can sit together as long as there is room for all the siblings. This may make some tables crowded, but it will help with cooperation.

2. Explain to the children that they are planning a surprise for their parents. Tell them that lots of times their parents do not realize what good people they are, and how much they do for their children. At this very moment, their parents are watching a video about how important parenting is. They are going to help their parents understand this and show them how much they are appreciated. Actually, most parents are saints.

3. **"Where do you see pictures of saints?"** Give the children time to explore this. If you live in an area where most of the churches are fairly new, children may have no experience of stained glass windows with saints in them. If yours is an older church with saint windows, or there is one in the area with which the children may be familiar, remind them of the saints in the windows.

4. **"Usually, when we see saints in windows, they are doing something or have special symbols. When you see Saint Elizabeth Seton, you usually see her with poor children, because she started a school for the poor. When you see Saint Francis, you see him with animals because he talked to the animals and they came to him, even the wildest, and sat and listened. You see Saint John Bosco with young boys. Why do you think that is so? Why do they show Saint Thomas Aquinas with books?"**

5. Take whatever time you need to help the children see that we picture saints with the things they did that we connect with their holiness.

6. **"What are some of the wonderful things your parents do for you?"**

7. Write the ideas on a board, so that children can see them and choose, if they can't think of something for their own parents.

8. **"If someone were going to put your mom or your dad or both in a stained glass window, what would they be doing in the window?"**

9. Explain that they are going to make windows for the parents who came with them tonight. If both parents came, both go in the windows. If there is more than one child from a family, one could make a window for Mom and one for Dad.

10. On the line at the bottom of the window, they are to print their parent's saint name. "Saint" will already be printed on the window, and they have their parents' names printed on the cards. Stop and do this, asking older siblings to help little ones.

11. In the circle in the center, they are to draw or paste a picture from a magazine, one or more of the important things their parents do for them.

12. When they are finished, they turn the window over and glue cellophane sheets over the openings in the template. It may be necessary to cut some of the sheets. Little ones will need a great deal of support for this second part of the task.

13. When they are finished, staple a string to the top of each window for hanging purposes. Ask each child his or her parent's saint name. Take time for each family of siblings to respond, because you want them to be able to do that as part of the closing. Explain to them that you will be doing a litany of the saints at the closing. They will all stand in the sanctuary, holding their windows, and will say their parent's names one at a time.

14. Collect the windows, keeping siblings' windows together. It is helpful if the different leaders collect their own groups, since it will make them easier to give back. Tell the children to take the index cards and give them back to their parents.

CLOSING

1. Bring the children back to the group.

2. Point out to the group as a whole that part of the reason we have lost the sense of our own holiness is because we don't have enough "ordinary" saints.

3. Ask them what you need to be canonized. Someone will know that you need miracles, alleged and confirmed.

4. Explain that we often don't see the miracles in our lives because we dismiss ordinary miracles and only look for big ones. "**A miracle is something that could not happen without the intervention of God.**" For many of the parents there, point out it was a miracle they got there.

5. "**We all have miracles in your lives. Your children have been talking about how wonderful you are, and all your miracles. Talk with them, and with one other family, and come up with your miracles. Also, name two people who will fight for your canonization in Rome. Who are the people who know you are holy?**"

6. Give about five minutes for the discussion. Then explain that it is time for the canonization.

7. Invite the children to stand and lay hands on their parents. Explain that you would not think of canonizing them in your own words. You are relying on the word of God.

8. Open the Bible, stretch one hand over the people. The leader does the reading.

9. Read Colossians 3:12-15 from the "old" Jerusalem Bible translation.

10. Close the Bible and end by saying: "**And may the God who creates, the God who redeems, and the God who has made all of us holy, bless us and remain with us forever and ever.**"

11. Ask the parents to write "Saint" in front of their names on the cards, and ask them to congratulate one another.

12. While they are doing that, call the children out, give them their windows, and have them line up in front of the adults—across the sanctuary if you are in church, or across the front of the hall.

13. You are going to end with a litany of the saints, but many adults no longer know the responses to the first part of the litany. Keep it simple, the way the responses are done at Mass. Simply lead strongly when the response changes to "Pray for us." Let the children know they are to say their parents' names when you point to them.

LITANY OF THE SAINTS

"**Please stand and let us end with a litany of the new saints**":

L. "**Lord, have mercy on us.**"
R. "Lord, have mercy on us."

L. "**Christ, have mercy on us.**"
R. "Christ, have mercy on us."

L. "**Lord, have mercy on us.**"
R. "Lord, have mercy on us."

L. "**Holy Mary**"
R. "Pray for us."

L. "**Saint Joseph**"
R. "Pray for us."

L. "**(Patron of your church)**"
R. "Pray for us."

Point to first group of siblings who say parents' saint name(s). All respond "Pray for us." Continue until all the "saints" have been named.

"Let us pray:

Loving God,
    when you sent your Son to the world,
    you sent him as a baby to a family.

Mary and Joseph taught him to walk,
    to talk, to pray.

They found joy in each new step,
    loved him, and became a holy family
    doing ordinary, everyday things.

Remind us that we, too,
    are called to extraordinary holiness
    in a thousand ordinary ways.

Bless all our families
    and keep us close to you and to each other.

We ask this as we ask all things,
    in the name of Jesus our brother. Amen."

ADVENT WREATHS

OVERVIEW

An Advent wreath is a green, circular wreath with three purple candles and one pink candle. The candles represent the four thousand years the world waited for a Savior. A new candle is lit, and a prayer of preparation recited, each Sunday. The pink candle is lighted on the third Sunday, Gaudete Sunday, when the readings anticipate the joy of the birth of Jesus.

Advent wreaths are a wonderful way to celebrate Advent in the home and to introduce family prayer. Many families enjoy saying the prayer and lighting the candles all week long. The following activity is designed to encourage families to celebrate with the wreaths by giving them the opportunity to make them together. It will be necessary to have the families sign up in advance so that you will know how much material you will need.

Charging for the day may make it easier for the parish to provide the materials, and will elicit a firmer commitment from the families.

MATERIALS

- Foam or sponge florist rings (one for each family)
- Cones, evergreens for decorating
- A box of Advent candles for each family
- Bowl of holy water
- A large candle
- Copies for each family of the prayers for lighting the wreath

REMOTE PREPARATION

1. Gather the materials. We have found that the easiest wreaths are made out of Styrofoam™ rings or florist sponge rings sold at craft stores, cutting holes for the candles and sticking greens and cones into the ring. You may want to try the straw rings or something more elaborate. Try making one first so that you are certain everyone will be able to do it.

2. Set up stations for each family, with rings (for the wreath), candles (if you cannot get the traditional three purple and one pink, use white with purple and pink ribbon), evergreens, and small pine cones. It is helpful to have families working close to each other, two or three to a table.

3. Ask the families to bring a small knife for cutting the foam, and refreshments to share. Invite any that have access to evergreens or pine cones to bring those also.

4. Place a bowl of water and a candle in the church, or in an area where the families will meet to pray and bless their wreaths.

5. Prayers for use in lighting the Advent wreath candles are given in most missalettes. A simpler prayer, written with families in mind, is given at the end of this experience. You may wish to prepare copies of the prayer to give to each family.

6. Prepare a reader.

EXPERIENCE

1. As the families arrive, assign them to work spots. Be sure to let families who want to work together have that opportunity. This will keep the children happy and occupied.

2. Explain the meaning of the Advent wreath and how to make them. It is helpful to have one already finished for people to use as a model.

3. When everyone has finished making the wreaths, gather everyone around the altar (or place designated for prayer) holding their wreaths.

Leader: "Just as the world
 waited in darkness for the Messiah,
 the light of the world,
 we wait in the ever-darkening
 days of winter for the feast of his birth
 and for the day when he will come
 again." (Leader lights the candle.)

Reader: Isaiah 9:2-3

Leader: "Lord, bless our Advent prayer.
 Give each of us the courage
 to make your light shine forth
 in the world. We ask this…
 (leader dips thumb in bowl of water and traces cross on own Advent wreath while saying)
 …in the name of the Father, the Son, and the Holy Spirit. Amen."
 (The bowl of water is then passed around and one member of the family holds it while another dips his/her thumb in the water and traces a cross on the wreath while saying the blessing out loud.)

Leader: "Lord, we gather with
 all those who waited one thousand years
 for your coming. Come, Lord Jesus."

All: "Come and be born in our hearts."

Leader lights one candle of his/her own wreath from the candle on the altar, then passes the taper to the first family on the right. The person who lights the candle says: "**Come, Lord Jesus**" and the family responds: "**Come and be born in our hearts.**"

4. Close by singing an Advent song.

5. End with refreshments.

ADVENT WREATH FAMILY PRAYERS

First Week

> All: "Lord, we wait with all those who waited one thousand years for your coming."
>
> Leader: "Come, Lord Jesus,"
>
> All: "Come and be born in our hearts."
>
> Leader: "Isaiah, you promised the Messiah would come as a light to shine in our darkness."
>
> All: "Teach us to wait patiently and prepare joyfully."
> (Light one purple candle.)

Second Week

> All: "Lord, we wait with all those who waited two thousand years for your coming."
>
> Leader: "Come, Lord Jesus,"
>
> All: "Come and be born in our hearts."
>
> Leader: "John, you cried out in the wilderness, preparing the world for Jesus."
>
> All: "Teach us to wait patiently and prepare joyfully."
> (Light two purple candles.)

Third Week

> All: "Lord, we wait with all those who waited three thousand years for your coming."
>
> Leader: "Come, Lord Jesus,"
>
> All: "Come and be born in our hearts."
>
> Leader: "Joseph, you trusted Mary, supporting and protecting her."
>
> All: "Teach us to wait patiently and prepare joyfully."
> (Light two purple candles and the pink candle.)

Fourth Week

> All: "Lord, we wait with all those who waited four thousand years for your coming."
>
> Leader: "Come, Lord Jesus,"
>
> All: "Come and be born in our hearts."
>
> Leader: "Mary, you carried the Christ within you."
>
> All: "Teach us to wait patiently and prepare joyfully."
> (Light all four candles.)

JESSE TREES

OVERVIEW

A Jesse tree is a bare branch that holds symbols of all the people who waited and prepared for the coming of the Messiah. It is this love and preparation that make flowers burst forth from the branch, and this is why a stark branch, rather than an evergreen tree, is used.

MATERIALS

- Several small bare branches potted in coffee cans
- One large potted branch for parish tree
- Clear plastic sheets for making symbols (transparencies work well)
- Magic markers
- Bibles
- List of characters
- Possible symbols of biblical characters
- Plain paper
- Index cards
- basket
- Christmas tree hooks
- Bowl of water
- Evergreen branch
- Small table
- Candle

REMOTE PREPARATION

1. Invite families of the parish to the celebration, and ask each family to bring a bare branch potted in a can about the size of a coffee can. Have several cans and bare branches ready in case some families forget to bring them. Pot a large barren branch for a parish Jesse tree.

2. Prepare a work space for each family, with a Bible and a list of the characters and Scripture references given here. Because some of the references are quite long, give a simple explanation for each. If you are artistic, you may also want to include a drawing of a possible symbol for each character.

3. Families will be making symbols for all the people who waited for Jesus. Decide on what you will use for the symbols. We found clear plastic sheets worked well. This allowed parents to draw symbols on paper and little ones to trace and color. Parents could then cut them out. We used Christmas tree hooks to hang the symbols. If you give the parents drawn symbols, this makes the activity even easier. Cardboard, aluminum foil, or dough will all work well, the more durable the better. Choose a medium with which you are comfortable, then place the needed materials at each family station.

4. Place the names of each of the persons on the list of Scripture characters on separate cards, and put them in a basket.

5. Prepare a central area for prayer, preferably in the church or a separate room from where you have been working. Place a bowl of water and candle on the altar or center table, and a large evergreen branch for sprinkling.

EXPERIENCE

1. Gather with an Advent song.

2. Explain to the families the meaning of a Jesse tree. Point out that they have been given a list of the names of some of the people who waited for Jesus.

3. They will be making symbols for those people for their Jesse trees. They will not have time to do them all, but they can finish at home.

4. Each family will also be asked to make one symbol for the parish Jesse tree. Hold out the basket with the names in it, and ask one member from each family to come forward and pull a name. That is the symbol they will make. They are to designate one person to carry the symbol, and one person to prepare one sentence about this person to share with the rest of the group.

5. The families may not feel comfortable looking up the Scripture. That is why it is important to have a simple explanation for each character.

6. After the families have had approximately 45 minutes to work, point out that each of us is also waiting for the Lord. Ask them to make a symbol for their own family to hang on the parish tree, and designate one person to hang it. Allow another 15 minutes for this activity.

7. When everyone has their family symbol and their parish symbol ready, ask the families to try to get in order chronologically, according to the character they were asked to make for the parish tree. Adam and Eve will be easy, and so will Mary and Joseph, but the others may require some help. It does not have to be completely accurate; it is just meant to be fun.

LIST OF CHARACTERS

PERSON	**SCRIPTURE**	**SYMBOL**
Adam and Eve	Genesis 3	the apple
Noah	Genesis 7	the ark or rainbow
Abraham	Genesis 12ff	camel
Sarah	Genesis 12ff	tent
Isaac	Genesis 21;22	ram
Rebecca	Genesis 24:19-28; 27:1ff	well
Jacob	Genesis 28:10-22	ladder
Rachel and Leah	Genesis 29:15-30	veil
Joseph	Genesis 39-48	coat of many colors
Moses	Exodus	tablets for commandments
Miriam	Exodus 15:20-21	small stringed instrument
David	1 Samuel 16:1-16	harp
Solomon	1 Kings 3:4-15	crown
Ruth	Book of Ruth	anchor (for faithfulness)
Isaiah	Isaiah 11:1-9	lion and lamb
Deborah	Judges 4	tent peg and mallet
Joshua	Joshua 6:1-15	trumpet
Daniel	Daniel 6:17-24	lion in cage
Elizabeth	Luke 1:39-55	small home
Zechariah	Luke 1:5-25	temple or altar
Mary	Luke 1:26-38	lily
Joseph	Matthew 1:18-25	hammer or saw
Jesus	Luke 2:1-20	Chi-Rho

CLOSING

Process into the area designated for prayer, with the first person carrying the parish Jesse tree, followed by a person carrying the Scriptures, and finally by the families carrying their own trees, and in historical order. The leader of prayer or celebrant walks last.

Entrance song: "O Come O Come, Emmanuel"

The potted tree is placed in the center of the sanctuary. Those designated to carry the symbols gather around it in a semicircle, facing the congregation; those reading the one line descriptions stand behind them.

Celebrant: **"We gather with all those who first awaited the coming of the Messiah, knowing we also are numbered among those who wait in joyful hope.**

Let us pray:

**Loving and present God,
we remember those who longed for
the coming of your Son.
Bless our barren tree.
Let it be for us a reminder
to prepare a place in our hearts
so that we might recognize Jesus
every place we meet him in our lives."**
Celebrant sprinkles water in the form of a cross on the tree, saying
"In the name of the Father, and of the Son, and of the Holy Spirit."

All: **"Amen."**

Reading: Isaiah 11:1-9

Celebrant: **"Isaiah painted a picture
of the coming of the Messiah.
Let us remember
all those who waited in joyful hope."**

(The celebrant reads the list of names. As he/she reads each name, the person carrying the symbol steps forward and hangs it on the tree. The reader for the family group reads the one line describing the person, then both return to their family in the pews.)

When all have returned to their seats, the celebrant asks:

Celebrant: **"Is there anyone here
who waits for the Lord?"**

The person designated in each family or household (and it can be two or three when all the children want to do it) comes forward, hangs their family symbol on the tree, and says: **"The N. Family waits for the Lord."**

When all have finished, the celebrant invites the families to lift their own trees, and he proceeds down the aisle blessing them with the branch while the families sing a song of blessing.

Song: "River of Glory" by Dan Schutte

Celebrant: **"Let us offer one another a sign of God's peace."**

Closing song: "Send Us Your Spirit" by Dan Schutte

SACRAMENT SCAVENGER HUNT

OVERVIEW

This lesson can be used quite successfully for sacramental preparation programs, particularly Eucharist and Confirmation, as a whole family experience to close a year on the study of sacraments, or as part of a family retreat that takes place in a church setting.

The entire experience will take approximately two hours, depending on the ages of the children involved.

MATERIALS

- Colored index cards, one for each family, different colors for each group or team
- Seven large (e.g., 8.5″ x 11″) cards for each team

REMOTE PREPARATION

1. You will be dividing into intergenerational groups for this experience. If you are doing this with families not already in some type of group, have as many different colored index cards as you plan to have teams (five to six families is a good sized group). Hand a colored index card to each family as they enter. The color will signify their group.

2. Each team will need one large card (8.5″ x 11″) *for each sacrament*. At the top of the card, put the name of the sacrament. Make three columns. At the top of the first column, put "symbol"; at the top of the second, put "found"; at the top of the third, put "reason." Make sure you have seven large cards for each team.

3. Walk around the church and look for all the symbols you can find for each of the sacraments. It would be helpful to leave some in strange places, such as a stole in one of the pews, etc. Leave out a ciborium and altar bread in the sacristy, a stole in the reconciliation room, etc. Make your own list of symbols that you find in the church.

4. Have pencils for each group. If your groups are large, it may be helpful to have more than one scavenger card per sacrament for each team.

EXPERIENCE

1. Welcome the families in the main body of the church. Begin with a song about symbols and sacraments, such as "Anthem."

2. Ask the group to search through their persons, pockets, and pocketbooks and see if they can find anything that might be considered a "symbol." Families that have been focusing on sacraments will be quick to point out things that might be conceived as symbols, even though they may not be seen that way originally. If the group has difficulty getting started, offer some ideas, e.g., wedding ring—symbol of love, car keys—symbol of freedom, pictures—symbol of family, jewelry gifts—symbol of love or friendship, driver's license—symbol of maturity.

3. **"We belong to a Church that prays in symbols and symbolic actions. What are the symbolic actions we have been studying this year?"**

4. **"Our rituals are supplemented by many different symbols. Today, we are going to have a scavenger hunt for symbols."**

5. Give each group a card for each sacrament. (All groups will have seven cards.) The groups can divide up the work in any way they wish. The object of the hunt is to find as many symbols for each sacrament as they can. They must name the symbol, where they found it, and if it is an "odd" symbol that may not be accepted by the group, give their reasons for choosing it. (For example, a group may choose the door as a symbol of baptism, because it is an entrance.)

6. Allow at least forty-five minutes, longer if the families are young. Ring a bell to signify that time is up.

7. Ask the first group to tell the symbols they found for baptism. The other groups should check any of the symbols they have. When the first ones are finished, ask the rest of the groups for any symbols that were missed. If a group disagrees strongly with the choice of a particular object as a symbol for that sacrament, the finding team must explain their choice. If the group still disagrees, that symbol is discounted. When all the symbols are accounted for, see which team has discovered the most. They get one point.

8. Ask the next team to share the symbols they found for confirmation. Continue until all the symbols have been shared and there is a winner for each sacrament.

9. If the groups have missed some obvious symbols (safe on the wall where the oils are kept, the community being themselves, sanctuary lamp, stations of the cross), review them.

10. If some of the groups choose some very unusual symbols, go back over those. Explaining choices of symbols will reveal a great deal about how people think about sacraments.

11. Close with refreshments.

FORGIVENESS

OVERVIEW

The following family activity was originally designed to help those families who are preparing a child for the sacrament of reconciliation for the first time. It has been modified here, to review the concept of forgiveness and celebrate reconciliation outside the sacrament. It makes an excellent preparation for Lent.

MATERIALS

- White paper plates (one for each person)
- Magic markers or crayons
- String

REMOTE PREPARATION

1. You will be making masks. Prepare an area for each family with paper plates for masks (enough for each family member to make one), crayons or magic markers, string for tying the masks on.

2. Prepare four teens to mime the story, in Genesis 3:1-7, of the temptation of Adam and Eve. Actually begin the mime with creation, with one teen acting as God. Then have one teen act as the serpent in the temptation. Have them wear tan leotards (for being "naked") and cover themselves with green cloth or leaves.

3. This activity takes place in two separate areas. It begins in a hall, and ends in the church or an area that can be set up for prayer.

EXPERIENCE

1. Opening: Choose a gathering song your families know and like.

2. Mime: The mime begins in semi darkness, with Adam and Eve lying on the floor.

   - **"After God had created the world, God took clay of the earth and made a man."** God lifts Adam up and works at "making" him.

   - **"God breathed into Adam, and Adam became a living person."** God breathes into Adam and Adam begins to dance. As he looks around, his dance gets slower and he begins to droop sadly.

   - **"Adam was lonely, and so God created Eve to be his mate, his equal in all things, his companion."** God raises Eve from the floor then leaves as the two dance together.

   - **"God gave Adam and Eve a garden, and told them they could eat anything except the fruit from the tree of the knowledge of good and evil."** Adam and Eve look at a make-believe tree.

   - **"The serpent came and tempted Eve to try the fruit."** Serpent slithers out and picks fruit off the tree, offering it to Eve.

   - **"Eve tasted the fruit and shared it with Adam."** Eve offers fruit and Adam eats. They look down at themselves, and hurry to the side to clothe themselves in leaves.

   - **"And when they had eaten the forbidden fruit, they saw they were naked and covered themselves."** Adam and Eve leave.

3. **"After Adam and Eve sinned, they covered themselves. Whenever we sin, we cover up the beautiful people God created us to be. Think about that for a minute. Sometimes we cover up our honesty by lying, our kindness by selfishness, our respect by rudeness."**

4. Invite the group to think of ways we cover up the good people God made us to be. Have them share their answers.

5. **"When we sin, we put on a mask that hides who we really are called to be. Most of us have favorite masks, things we are most apt to do that hide what good people we are. Think about yourself for a few minutes. What do you do that you would most like to change? What is the mask you wear that hides the beautiful person you are?"**

6. Have the group break up into families. Each person is to make a mask that represents the thing they are most apt to do to cover up their goodness, the thing they would most like to change. Have a sample mask prepared to show everyone. Encourage children to look for the *most important* way they cover up the good people they are. Allow enough time for the majority of people to finish (20-30 minutes), then have everyone go to the church, or the area set aside for prayer, wearing the masks.

7. Once the group has gathered, the leader should ask: **"What would it be like if all of us wore masks all the time?"**

8. Give the group a chance to explore the fact that we would never know who one another truly was.

9. Point out that sometimes it is hard to give up our masks. Do *not* ask children if they find it difficult, because that is not something they want to admit.

10. **"Sometimes we hide behind our masks because we are afraid people will not love us anymore."**

11. Explain that Jesus gave us a story about how God feels when we fail. Tell the story of the Prodigal Son very simply, being sure to ask if they have ever been lost, and how they felt when they were found.

12. **"God is always ready to welcome us back. We just have to be willing to give up our masks."**

13. **"We are going to take time this evening to ask God's forgiveness for all the ways we fail to be the beautiful people we were meant to be."**

CLOSING PRAYER

Begin with gentle, reflective music.

Invitation to Prayer: "'**Forgiveness**' …
      an invitation…
      to become people who are forgiving…
      people who see themselves as gift…
      who are not afraid to be who they are."

Prayer: "**Loving God,
      we come to you to ask your mercy and your help.
      Free us from our masks.
      Help us to be the beautiful people you created us to be.**"

Reading: 2 Corinthians 5:17-18

Leader: "**God calls us to
      help one another be reconciled.
      Turn to the ones near you,
      offer them the peace of Christ,
      and take off their mask.**"

Give the community time to remove one another's masks and to wish each other peace.

Leader: "**Jesus taught us that
      we would be forgiven
      as we forgive others.
      Let us say the prayer Jesus gave us.**"

Pray the Lord's Prayer.

Close with an appropriate song, such as "Take This Mask" by Michael Avolicino.

End with refreshments. Encourage the families to take the masks home and hang them up as a reminder of the evil they are trying to avoid in their lives. If the activity is done as a lenten activity, ask them to try to give up the mask for Lent.

LENTEN CROSSES

OVERVIEW

This activity is similar to Advent wreaths. It was developed by a family in our program, and has become a tradition for many parishes and families since then. The original families made their crosses out of wood, many of them using part of the Christmas tree trunk, cutting it in half and notching it so that the cross can lie flat. It can be done that way in the parish, but it will require power tools and more preparation. For this reason, Styrofoam™ crosses are recommended here.

The entire activity will take less than an hour. It can be done in conjunction with the prayer service on mercy (page 134), if you have more time.

MATERIALS

- Pieces of Styrofoam™ for making crosses, 2 inches thick, dark color if possible
- Small twigs, thorns, to decorate crosses
- Five purple candles and one pink for each family
- Lenten prayer cards for each family
- Glue or pins

REMOTE PREPARATION

1. Cut the Styrofoam™ into pieces, 12 inches long and 2½ inches wide, for the vertical bar of the cross. Cut the horizontal piece the same width and 6 inches long. Carve a 1 inch deep indent in each bar, to allow the horizontal piece to lie flat on the vertical piece.

2. Prepare an area for each family, with a vertical and horizontal beam, twigs, dry weeds, thorns, and candles.

3. If it has not been possible to get dark foam, provide dark markers, purple or brown, to color it.

4. Write out the lenten prayer given at the end of this activity for every family.

5. Put one of the crosses together yourself, marking the holes for the candles, carving them out, putting the cross together and gluing or pinning it, and adding the decorations. Take careful note of any problems you encounter. If you have someone who is good with crafts, seek his or her help in working out any kinks.

EXPERIENCE

1. Explain to the families that we are going to make lenten crosses in the same manner that we made Advent wreaths. Show them the bars for the cross, and demonstrate how the cross is to be put together.

2. Ask the group how many weeks there are in Lent, and point out the six candles. Explain that purple represents repentance, which is the focus of Lent, and that the pink candle is for the fourth Sunday. Just as, in Advent, the joy of the coming feast broke through the solemn preparation, so it does in Lent, this time on what is known as Laetare Sunday.

3. Share your own finished cross, and explain any difficulties you had.

4. Ask the families to make their crosses, then to agree on one thing that they will do as a family for Lent. They are going to be asked to name their promise in the candle blessing. Give them the opportunity to find a comfortable way to name it.

CLOSING PRAYER

1. Prayer: "**Lord, throughout these forty days, we want to walk with you. Bless this cross as a reminder of this sacred time. Help us to be true to the lenten promises we have made. We ask this in the name of the Father, the Son, and the Holy Spirit.**"

2. The leader traces a cross with holy water on the candle-cross saying: "**Lord help me to be faithful to…**(names lenten promise), **in the name of the Father, and of the Son, and of the Holy Spirit. Amen.**"

3. The leader passes the dish of holy water to the first family. They bless their cross, saying simply: "**Lord, help us to be faithful to…**(lenten promise), **in the name of the Father, and of the Son, and of the Holy Spirit. Amen.**"

4. Prayer: "**Lord, help us to be faithful to prayer this Lent so that we may become a light in the darkness.**"

5. The leader lights one purple candle, then takes a taper and lights it from the candle, and hands it to the first family. They light one purple candle, praying: "**Lord, help us to be faithful to prayer this Lent so that we may become a light in the darkness.**"

6. Close with a lenten hymn that all the families know.

7. Give the families the lenten prayer cards, and invite them to light their candles every Sunday.

PRAYERS FOR LIGHTING THE LENTEN CANDLE

It is suggested that you use the readings for the liturgical year you are celebrating.

First Sunday of Lent

Leader: "**Remember your mercies to us, O Lord.**"

Response: "**Teach us to show mercy to others.**"
The first lenten candle is lighted.

Reading: Cycle A—Matthew 4:1-11
Cycle B—Genesis 9:8-15
Cycle C—Luke 4:1-13

Leader: "**Lord, help us to be people of prayer.**"

Response: "**Lord, help us to be people of prayer.**"

Second Sunday of Lent

Leader: "**Remember your mercies to us, O Lord.**"

Response: "**Teach us to show mercy to others.**"
Two purple candles are lighted.

Reading: Cycle A—Matthew 17:1-9
Cycle B—Romans 8:31-34
Cycle C—Genesis 15:5-12

Leader: "**Lord, help us to be people who listen.**"

Response: "**Lord, help us to be people who listen.**"

Third Sunday of Lent

Leader: "**Remember your mercies to us, O Lord.**"

Response: "**Teach us to show mercy to others.**"
Three purple candles are lighted.

Reading: Cycle A—Exodus 17:3-7
Cycle B—John 2:13-25
Cycle C—Luke 13:6-9

Leader: "**Lord, help us to be people of faith.**"

Response: "**Lord, help us to be people of faith.**"

FOURTH SUNDAY OF LENT

    Leader: **"Remember your mercies to us, O Lord."**

Response: **"Teach us to show mercy to others."**
Three purple candles and one pink candle are lighted.

Reading: Cycle A—1 Samuel 16:6-13
Cycle B—John 9:1-41
Cycle C—Luke 15:11-32

    Leader: **"Lord, help us to be people of forgiveness."**

Response: **"Lord, help us to be people of forgiveness."**

FIFTH SUNDAY OF LENT

    Leader: **"Remember your mercies to us, O Lord."**

Response: **"Teach us to show mercy to others."**
Four purple candles and one pink candle are lighted.

Reading: Cycle A—John 11:1-45
(or tell the story, if children are small)
Cycle B—Jeremiah 31:31-34
Cycle C—Isaiah 43:16-21

    Leader: **"Lord, help us to be people of life."**

Response: **"Lord, help us to be people of life."**

PASSION SUNDAY

    Leader: **"Remember your mercies to us, O Lord."**

Response: **"Teach us to show mercy to others."**
All six candles are lighted.

Reading: John 12:12-16

    Leader: **"Lord, help us to be people of love."**

Response: **"Lord, help us to be people of love."**

CALVARY WALK

OVERVIEW

This reflection on the Way of the Cross was designed to help families recognize how Jesus is suffering in the world today. Although preschoolers can easily be incorporated into the activity, it is not particularly appropriate for those families who only have small children. School age children will gain far more from the experience.

MATERIALS

- 14 large cardboard crosses (we used boxes from appliance stores as they made sturdier crosses)
- Newspapers, news magazines, mission magazines, general magazines
- Glue
- Scissors
- Pencils
- Paper with outline for prayer
- Scrap paper
- Magic markers
- Flashlights and extra batteries
- 14 Way of the Cross booklets (these are simply for the names of the stations and need not be the same ones for each group)
- Large rough wooden cross, 6 feet or more

REMOTE PREPARATION

1. Prepare the 14 crosses out of heavy cardboard. The crosses need to be large, roughly three feet by four feet. Number them in Roman numerals.

2. If your parish does not have a plain wooden cross, have someone build one for you.

3. Prepare a "prayer page" for each of the 14 groups with the following three prompts (and space to respond):

    ▶ How Jesus suffered in this station: _____
    ▶ How Jesus continues to suffer in this manner in the world today: _____
    ▶ Prayer: _____

4. Prepare a simple talk, describing the passion and death of Jesus, but carefully pointing out that when Jesus became human, he took on all our suffering. Whenever anyone suffers in the world today, we are seeing the passion of Jesus all over again.

5. Prepare 14 work stations. Each will need glue, a prayer page, pencils, several newspapers and magazines, and scissors. Place the 14 numbered crosses across the front of the sanctuary.

6. Decide how you will divide the families into 14 groups. You may want to give a card with a number on it to each family as they enter the church. If families want to work together, give them the same numbers.

7. Decide in advance how you plan to pray the Way of the Cross. If you plan to invite other parishioners, you will need to make an announcement in the bulletin at least two weeks in advance. Two ways to celebrate are given here.

8. Joe Wise has a beautiful song called "Remember Me" that would be very appropriate to have playing in the background while the families are gathering and working.

EXPERIENCE

1. When all the families are assembled in church, lower the lights (if it is possible to make your church somewhat dark at midday), sing a simple song of the passion that most people know, such as "Were You There," while one person walks slowly down the aisle bearing the large cross and stands it in the center of the sanctuary.

2. Prayer:
   "Loving God,
   we gather together today
   not only to remember how Jesus
   suffered and died for us once,
   but how he continues to suffer and die
   in our world today.
   Help us to be always aware
   that to 'remember' Jesus
   is not just to call him to mind,
   but to re-member,
   to put together again,
   the broken body of Christ
   we find all around us."

3. Describe the passion and death simply, going through the Way of the Cross, even pointing out the stations as you do it (maximum 10 minutes).

4. When you have finished, explain to the group that we are all the body of Christ and many members of that body are still suffering in the world today. Point to the first station, and ask if anyone can explain how Jesus might still be unjustly condemned to die in our world today.

5. Explain that their job today is to write a contemporary Way of the Cross. Each family has been given a number, and they will be working on that station. They are going to explain what happened in that station first, then how Jesus continues to suffer in our world in that manner. They will then choose pictures and words to glue on their cross to demonstrate that suffering and, finally, write a prayer for the suffering members of the body of Christ that they are re-membering.

6. Hold up the first cross, and have those families assigned to that group come and take that cross to the hall. Tell them to take time to introduce themselves. Do the same with the other crosses.

7. Float among the groups and help them to choose a contemporary topic. Try to get the groups to choose different ones. We have not found this to be too much of a problem.

8. Ask the groups to decide who will read each of the three parts of the prayer, and to practice them. They will need to be read *loudly* so that everyone can hear. Also ask for one person in each group to lead the Lord's Prayer, the Hail Mary, and the Glory Be…—to be recited at the end of each station.

CLOSING CELEBRATION

The closing Way of the Cross can be simply for the families who participated, or the rest of the parish can be invited to join at a particular time. We have found it works best if it is done in at least partial darkness with flashlights, outside when possible. If you are planning to do the Way of the Cross with the whole parish, give your families a chance to do it first.

For the Families

1. Set up the crosses at 14 spots around the inside or outside of the church. You will probably want one person to hold each cross.

2. Form a procession behind one person carrying the large cross. You will be saying the three traditional prayers (Lord's Prayer, Hail Mary, Glory Be…) as you walk. As leader, you begin saying them as the group walks to the first station. At that station, the group that prepared it does the reading as planned, then the person chosen to lead the traditional prayers begins the three prayers as the entire group walks to the second station. This is repeated at each station.

3. Our families did not like ending with the tomb, so we always finished with a "fifteenth station" at the baptismal font and read one of the Easter stories. We also included a commitment to some form of social action at the fifteenth station.

For the Parish

1. If you are planning to do the Way of the Cross for the entire parish, it is a good idea to give the families the opportunity to celebrate it first themselves. You may want to do that formally, as given above, or if time is short, simply have each group read what they have written for the station.

2. Have the families gather around the cross they prepared. If space is limited, you will need to limit the people to those who are reading and leading the prayers.

3. It may help to break parishioners into smaller groups and lead them through every 15 minutes. We have found if we advertise in this way, people do choose different times to come. This also allows several people to have the chance to be the cross bearer.

4. The stations are celebrated in the same manner as above, with the exception that the families are already by their station to read the description and prayer they have written. The people who are responsible for leading the three formal prayers after each station walk behind the group.

5. This evening should simply close with people leaving quietly. You may want to give them a small gift, such as a cross in the pocket, to carry with them as a reminder of their commitment to the suffering Christ in the world today.

EASTER EGG HUNT

OVERVIEW

This is a variation on the traditional Easter egg hunt. Its purpose is to have a good time while reviewing the concept of the new life we celebrate at Easter. While the main treasure that will be found in the eggs is not candy, you need to include some just to save disappointment. We use small jelly beans, and tell the teams they can be eaten as they are found.

This hunt was originally designed as an at-home activity. If you are doing this in a church setting, you will need to be creative about things like a "bed" (a blanket on a pew will do), a tub, etc.

REMOTE PREPARATION

1. You will need 36 large plastic eggs, divided into groups of six, each in a different color. If you are unable to get six different colors, make them by mixing halves. This way you would have a team of blue and red eggs, as well as a team of just blue or just red.

2. Clues for the hunt are provided here. Each group will have *six* eggs of one color. Each team will have a different color. Put one clue in each egg for each team. Put the number of the clue on a sticker on the outside of the egg. The first egg is given to the team. The other eggs will be hidden according to the directions.

3. Each team will need a basket for their eggs. Place the basket, the first egg, and a *New American Bible* in a separate area for each team.

4. You will need to have a small packet of seeds for each person. Enough packets for each team should be in the final egg, if they will fit, or wrapped in a box the same color as the eggs of each team. Egg or box should be marked with the number "6" and hidden in the number six spot on the list of clues.

5. As leader, you will want to *read through all the Scripture quotes*, and hide the rest of the eggs in the designated spots.

6. Plan in advance how you will divide families into teams. You may want to give each family a colored card that matches one of the egg colors as they enter the gathering space.

7. Ask six people, whom you know will be able to look up a Scripture reference, to act as your group leaders. Be careful not to assume that people come equipped with this knowledge.

8. If you suspect you will wind up with too many people on each team, you can form more teams by borrowing treasure hunt clues from the body of Christ experience (page 92). If you do not have enough people, simply eliminate a team.

9. Plan an area for prayer, in the church or in a large hall. Place the Easter candle in the center, and a large punch bowl of water.

CLUES

Team 1

1. Ephesians 1:22 - given to the team
2. 1 Corinthians 10:31 - near shoes, or anything to do with feet
3. Luke 7:32 - near food
4. Luke 6:44 - near organ, piano, musical instrument, or stereo
5. Mark 16:9 - near a tree, or in a bowl of fruit
6. This treasure is placed by a calendar

Team 2

1. 1 Corinthians 15:36-37 - given to team
2. Luke 5:18 - in a garden
3. Luke 5:37 - on couch or bed
4. Isaiah 44:3 - on a wine bottle
5. Mark 14:36 - by water of some kind
6. This treasure is placed by coffee cups

Team 3

1. Luke 4:11 - given to team
2. Mark 9:50 - on a stone
3. Isaiah 43:2 - near a salt shaker
4. Psalm 17:8 - near fireplace, grill, or candle
5. Ezekiel 34:13b - near bowl of apples
6. This treasure is hidden near water

Team 4

1. Ephesians 2:10 - given to team
2. Mark 14:18 - near art, a children's project (the word is "handiwork")
3. John 5:2 - at table for eating
4. Mark 12:41 - near a pool, or just near water if that is not possible
5. John 8:12 - near cash register, or baskets for collection on Sunday
6. This treasure is near a light

Team 5

1. Song of Songs 4:16 - given to team
2. 2 Corinthians 4:1 - in a garden
3. Psalm 3:5 - near a desk
4. Psalm 11:1 - by bed or couch
5. Luke 13:6 - by a bird feeder
6. This treasure is by a tree

Team 6

1. John 4:13 - given to team
2. Mark 1:33 by a faucet
3. Mark 6:38 - by a door
4. Luke 12:7 - on a loaf of bread
5. Daniel 3:21 - on a hairbrush in a bathroom
6. This treasure is in an oven

EXPERIENCE

1. Gather the families together and begin with a simple Easter song, such as "This Is the Day" by Michael Joncas.

2. Ask them what great feast we have just celebrated, and what we celebrate at Easter.

3. Show them an egg, and ask them why they think this is a symbol of Easter.

4. Once they have decided that it is because an egg is a symbol of new life, point out that the new life in an egg grows slowly and needs warmth and shelter to grow. The new life Jesus offers us in Easter also needs help to grow. Sometimes, it even takes some time to discover that new life in ourselves.

5. One of the ways we learn to discover that new life is through reading Scripture. Point out that today we are going to have a treasure hunt using Scripture.

6. In this treasure hunt, everyone will be looking for eggs. The color of the card they received as they entered is the color of their team, and the color eggs they will be looking for. Point out the designated leaders for each color team. Ask the families to join their leader in the designated spot, introduce themselves if some people do not know everyone, then listen to the directions.

7. Explain to the teams that they will find their first clue in the egg that is in their designated spot. They must look up the Scripture reference and see where it leads them. For example, if the reference led to "I am the bread of life, the next egg would probably be near a breadbox. Each egg contains the next clue, and special goodies which they can share during the hunt.

8. Explain in what areas the clues are hidden. Tell the groups they will get confused if they do not find them in order, and they cannot claim their treasure until they find all the clues. They may not disturb anyone else's eggs if they find them. The sixth egg or box of the same color contains the treasure. Tell the teams to bring it back unopened to the large group. Set them loose, but be prepared to help any group that gets too stuck.

9. When all the teams have found the treasure, gather them in the prayer space and invite them to open them.

CLOSING

Leader: **"Often, when we are given a treasure, it comes to us in seed form. What do we need to do to help it grow?"**
Allow the group to explore all the things necessary for a seed to grow.

Leader: **"What is the soil that helps our new life grow? What is the water, the sun?"**
Hopefully, the group will be able to come up with some metaphors for these, such as prayer and love and community.

Leader: **"Today, we are going to make a commitment to foster the new life we have been given through the death and Resurrection of Jesus."**
Light the Easter candle, lower the lights, and invite everyone to stand.

Leader: **"And so, let us repeat the promises we made at our baptism.
Do you reject Satan?"**

Response: **"I do."**

Leader: **"And all his works?"**

Response: **"I do."**

Leader: **"And all his empty promises?"**

Response: **"I do."**

Leader: **"Do you believe in God,
the Father almighty,
creator of heaven and earth?"**

Response: **"I do."**

Leader: **"Do you believe in Jesus Christ,
his only Son our Lord, who was born,
died, and rose for us?"**

Response: **"I do."**

Leader: **"Do you believe in the Holy Spirit?"**

Response: **"I do."**

Leader: **"Lord, bless this water."**
Leader extends hands over the water then lifts some up, allowing it to pour through the fingers.
"Let it become for us a sign of our baptism and of our commitment to live lives of…
(Use the words the group gave for all that is needed to make a seed grow. The leader blesses self, saying aloud the words of the sign of the cross.)
Bless these seeds as a sign of our commitment to new life."

Leader traces a cross on seed packet. Invite everyone to come forward, dip their hand in the water, trace a cross on their seed packet, and then bless themselves. Play soft music as this is happening.

By way of closing, sing "River of Glory" by Dan Schutte.

BODY OF CHRIST

The idea for this activity came from Sr. Joseph Marie Flynn, Hales Corner, Wisconsin.

OVERVIEW

The purpose of this activity is to remind us that we are all different parts of the body of Christ, and the body must work together in the world. It is appropriate as either a lenten or Easter season activity. It is an excellent family activity in preparation for First Eucharist. This activity is similar to the Easter Egg Hunt, and so it is recommended that you do these two in different years.

MATERIALS

- Wooden tapers for lighting candles
- 5 cardboard sheets
- "Clues" for each team
- 5 Bibles, NAB translation
- Scrap paper
- Pencils
- Tape
- Tea candles, one per person (the small candles that come in six packs with metal containers)
- Five or six large punch bowls

REMOTE PREPARATION

1. This experience takes a lot of preparation. Begin early.

2. Read the entire experience carefully. Read over the Scriptures in it several times, and reflect prayerfully on them, particularly the reading from 1 Corinthians. Practice reading it with great expression.

3. On one piece of cardboard, draw several mouths; on another, feet; on a third, hands; on a fourth, eyes; and on the last, ears. You can make the posters more interesting with socks and boots on the feet, muffs on the ears, mittens and gloves on the hands, etc. Cut each cardboard into 15 puzzle pieces. Keep the five puzzles separate. Each team will be finding the pieces to one of the puzzles and putting together one of the body parts, e.g., team 1 will find all the puzzle pieces that make up the eyes, etc.

4. You will be breaking into five teams. Each of the teams will need six clues on separate index cards. The clues for each team are given at the end of the lesson. Make out the index cards. Do them in different colors. (If the group is too large for five teams—maximum team size is six to seven families—create two puzzles for each of the body parts and two sets of clues. It is fairly easy to create clues, but it is possible to use the same clues if *every single* "team set" is clearly done in different colors, numbered differently, and hidden in different spots. For example, clues given for team 1 may also be used for a team 6.)

5. The first clue will be given to each team. The second clue will have the first three puzzle pieces clipped to it. The third clue will have the next three pieces. By the time a team has found all their clues, they will have 15 puzzle pieces.

6. Place the clues in the spots recommended beside them. If you do not have a comparable spot, read the *previous* clue, that is the one directing to that spot, and find some place the clue might also lead you. For example, John 6:35, "I am the bread of life," is meant to lead to the breadbox. If you are not meeting in a home, just put the clue with whatever snack is planned for after the activity. Carefully delineate the area in which clues will be hidden so that you can tell that to the groups.

7. Set up the hall with stations for each team, a circle of chairs, a large table for assembling the puzzle, a *New American Bible*, cellophane tape, the team's first clue.

8. In the church, or the area that will be used for prayer, set up several large punch bowls filled with water. Put the tea candles by the entrance the family will be using when the activity is over.

9. You will be dividing the families into teams by animal sounds. One team will be the pigs, one the cats, one the dogs, etc. Choose animals that make simple, recognizable sounds: horse, donkey, goose, hen, rooster, crow. If you have five teams, you will need five different animals. If you need to divide into more teams, you will need more animals. You will need to make out one card per family with the name of the animal that will indicate which team they are on.

10. Ask several adults, whom you know will be present, to assist in lighting the candles in the closing.

CLUES FOR PEACEMAKER TREASURE HUNT

Team 1

1. Mark 11:13 - to be given to the team
2. Exodus 17:6 - by a leafy plant
3. John 1:5 - by a water faucet
4. Acts 3:1 - on a light
5. John 12:3 - by a clock
6. Luke 14:34 - by a bottle of perfume or bath oil
7. Last clue - by a salt shaker

Team 2

1. Acts 2:35 - to be given to team
2. John 13:5 - by a footstool
3. Deuteronomy 6:9 - by a towel in the bathroom
4. Mark 6:43 - by a door
5. Mark 7:15 - in a wicker basket
6. Luke 21:18 - on a toilet
7. Last clue - by a hairbrush

Team 3

1. Acts 2:3 - to be given to the team
2. John 13:10 - by fireplace or candles
3. Ruth 3:4 - in bathtub or shower
4. Matthew 12:33 - on a bed
5. John 4:13 - in a fruit bowl
6. Acts 10:10 - by a faucet
7. Last clue - by refrigerator or food cupboard

Team 4

1. Daniel 3:21 - to be given to the team
2. John 9:5 - in an oven
3. Acts 7:58 - on a light
4. Luke 16:21 - by coats or in a coat closet
5. Genesis 28:12 - under the dining room table
6. Luke 12:3 - on a stairway
7. Last clue - by a closed door

Team 5

1. Joel 3:22 - to be given to the team
2. Isaiah 9:1 - on a leafy plant, or in a fruit bowl
3. Acts 20:9 - on a light or light switch
4. Luke 22:20 - on a window sill
5. Mark 2:15 - under a cup that resembles a chalice
6. Luke 7:32 - at a table
7. Last clue - by organ, piano, or some form of music

EXPERIENCE

1. As the families enter, give them the name of an animal. When all have arrived, explain that they are to find their work group by making the noise of the animal on the card they were given. They are to walk around and find other families making the same noise. When they think they have everyone, they should choose a work station and stand there, making the noise *very loudly* to insure that every family has found their group.

2. Ask everyone to make sure they know the names of everyone in the group. If the children know the adults, have them introduce them to each other, "This is Jimmy's mom," etc.

3. Invite everyone to be quiet and listen to the reading: 1 Corinthians 12:12-21.

4. This should be read with great expression, posing the questions in it as questions to the group. For example, the reader should ask "Can the eye say to the hand: I do not need you?"

5. When the reading is done, ask the group what we would do if the body were all just one part—a head, a mouth, a hand. **"Sometimes your mother may say you are all stomach, but we are all made up of many parts. Each of the parts has its own role. Each of us is a different part in the body of Christ."**

6. **"Today we are going to have a treasure hunt for the part of the mystical body that we are called to be."**

7. **"The clues to help us discover who we are were always in the Bible, and it is no different today. You have your first clue. It is a Scripture passage. Look up the passage and read it out loud to the group. It will tell you where the next clue is hidden. If the passage is about water, your next clue, and the first part of your puzzle, will be near water, etc. If it were the passage from John, 'I am the bread of life,' where would the next clue be? When you have found all of your clues, you will have the pieces of the puzzle that tell you what part of the body of Christ you are called to be right now. Put the puzzle together, and while you are doing that, I will come and give you another instruction."**

8. Make sure the group understands the directions; then give the signal to begin.

9. As everyone is putting the puzzle together (it may help to tape it to keep it stable), ask them to think of five ways that their particular body part works for good in the world. **"What do the hands of Christ do, what do the eyes of Christ do?"** Tell the groups you want them to put together a cheer for their part of the body of Christ.

10. When everyone is done, invite the groups to share their cheers. (You may need to walk around and encourage adults to participate in this part. Suggest old basketball cheers that might be redone to work.) Take time to applaud everyone's efforts.

11. Ask the families to choose one thing they honestly pledge themselves to do during this lenten/Easter season.

12. Invite everyone into the church. Ask them to walk quietly, and pick up a candle on the way in.

CLOSING

Leader: "**When did we become part of the body of Christ?**"

Response: Hopefully, many in the group will know it was at our baptism.

Leader: "**When we were baptized, we promised, or our godparents promised for us, to live as the body of Christ. Today, we renew those promises as members of the body of Christ.**"

Lower the lights and light the Easter candle or, if during Lent, a candle in the center of the altar.

Leader: "**Do you believe in God the Creator?**"

Response: "I do."

Leader: "**Do you believe in Jesus the Redeemer?**"

Response: "I do."

Leader: "**Do you believe in the Holy Spirit, the giver of life?**"

Response: "I do."

Leader: "**As hands of the body of Christ, what do you promise to do?**"

Response: Members of the group say the one thing their family promised to do. This will involve many people speaking at the same time, which is fine.

Leader: "**As feet of the body of Christ, what do you promise to do?**"

Response: Same as above.

Leader: "**As eyes of the body of Christ, what do you promise to do?**"

Response: Same as above.

Leader: "**As ears of the body of Christ, what do you promise to do?**"

Response: Same as above.

Leader: "**As mouths of the body of Christ, what do you promise to do?**"

Response: Same as above.

Leader: "**As a sign of our commitment and belonging in the body of Christ, bring your candle forward, light it, and put it in the water, saying the name of the church in which you were baptized, then return to your seat.**"

It will be important to have helpers at each bowl to help young people put their candles in gently and to relight any that get squelched.

Close by singing "We Are Many Parts" by Marty Haugen.

HOLY SPIRIT KITES

OVERVIEW

The purpose of this activity is to focus families on the action of the Holy Spirit in our lives. Throughout Scripture, the Spirit is portrayed as wind and breath and air. Building kites is a reminder that all good deeds are powered by the Spirit, as kites are powered by the wind.

If you wish a more formal ending, use the Holy Spirit Prayer on page 137.

MATERIALS

- kite kits
- kite string
- large meeting space
- open field wind and good weather

REMOTE PREPARATION

1. For this activity, you will need a general idea of the number of families so you can prepare accordingly. Set up areas for all families, with all the materials necessary for building the kites.

2. Make a copy of the "fruit of the Spirit" reading (Galatians 5:22-23) for each family.

3. Carefully prepare the reflection, and prepare two other people to do the two readings.

EXPERIENCE

Gathering Song: Gather families together with an opening song to the Holy Spirit. This can be done in church, if there is easy access to a large meeting space, or in the space where you will be making the kites.

Opening Prayer: **"Come Holy Spirit, fill the hearts of all of us. Recreate us and, through us, renew the earth."**

First Reading: Acts of the Apostles 2:1-4

Reflection: **"Who is the Holy Spirit?"**
(The Spirit is the very Spirit of Jesus, given to us so that we could all become like Jesus.)
"How did Jesus send the Spirit on Pentecost?"
(Leader should ask the questions and encourage answers. This is more effective if the leader walks among the families. The Spirit came as a strong wind and as tongues of fire.)
"How do we use the wind?"
(As a source of power—to drive windmills, and sailboats, and to fly kites. Encourage many answers, but help the group to discover wind is a source of power.)
"Just like the wind, the Holy Spirit is a source of power in all our lives. It is the Spirit that helps us to be gentle and kind and good. Chapter five of Galatians tells us how we will know the Spirit."

Second Reading: Galatians 5:22-23

Reflection: **"Whenever we see these things, 'fruit,' we know we are seeing the Holy Spirit in action. How many of them can you remember from the reading?"**
(After giving the group a chance to remember as many fruits as possible, the leader holds up a kite.)
"If the Spirit is wind, then we are kites. Without the Holy Spirit, we cannot fly." (Demonstrates.)
"But, you need more than a wind. What else do you need when you make a kite?"
(The group will probably suggest string and some may mention a tail, although many kites fly without them.)
"The string is what keeps the kite from flying away on its own. It connects the kite to the earth. If the Spirit is wind and we are the kites, the Church is the string. It keeps us connected."
(If you will be making tails for your kites, invite the group to reflect on the fact that tails provide balance, something we are usually given by our families and our communities.)

Kite Making: **"We will be going into the hall to make kites. You may want to put some of the fruit of the Spirit on them. Once we have them all made, we will go out to fly them."**
(Allow a good hour for kite flying, then bring everyone back for refreshments and a closing song to the Spirit.)

Alternative: If it is not possible to meet in a spot where the kites can be flown (and you will definitely want to make sure any open area you choose has enough wind to fly a kite), close the kite making with refreshments and a song to the Spirit. Plan to meet on another day, at a park, to fly the kites, or invite everyone to fly their kites on a family day of their own.

PART 4
RITUALS & PRAYER SERVICES

A COMMUNITY SHARES SYMBOLS

"Rituals are expressions of values and attitudes in the form of symbolic action."[4] Communities develop rituals for gathering and separating, for celebrating and for mourning, for forgiving and being forgiven. Through the ritual, a society not only acts out the sacred meaning symbolized in the action, it reminds its members to enter into the meaning. "The unity of a group, like all its cultural values, must find symbolic expression.... The symbol is at once a definite focus of interest, a means of communication, and a common ground of understanding."[5]

Every small community needs to develop rituals that help to identify the importance and meaning of the community for the members themselves. The beginning of this "symbolic action" lies in the use of symbol.

The root of "symbol" is the Greek word symbollein, "to match," and refers to an ancient custom. When an agreement was reached or a contract made in ancient Greece, it was customary to break something in two: a piece of pottery, a ring, a tablet. Each of the parties to the agreement was given one of the pieces or symbol. Either party could lay claim to their part of the agreement by presenting the symbol and connecting it to the other piece. The word eventually came to mean "recognition sign," e.g., the fish was a symbol by which the early Christians recognized one another.

Symbols became ways in which we understood ourselves and made that meaning known to others. Symbols are more than just signs, since they point to a meaning that is often beyond the power of words to express. Toynbee pointed out that a symbol does not reproduce that which it represents, it illuminates. It is an instrument to extend our vision, stimulate imagination and deepen our understanding.

Symbolic action is vital to any group working toward community. The first symbolic act of a group was discussed earlier and involved naming the group (page 12). A concrete symbol needs to be found that expresses the meaning of the name on a deeper level than words. A carefully chosen symbol is capable of carrying not only the value we assign it, but its own value and its own power to move us.

One intergenerational group named itself "Circles of Love," and chose as its symbol a set of wooden concentric circles, with each household represented by one of the circles. When the symbol was put together at the beginning of a meeting, it was intended to be instantly obvious if anyone was missing. The circle symbol also conveyed all the ancient meanings of "completeness," "no beginning or end," etc., but the wooden symbol itself made other things obvious. Cut with a jigsaw, the circles were not completely smooth and did not fit together easily, symbolic of the struggles the group faced as they worked toward community. In decorating the circles, several people wrapped ribbon around the outside of the wood, covering the circle and making the fit impossible. (Covering up, hiding true identity also works against community.) The circles had developed a message of their own, and as the group struggled to put them together each week, sanding down rough edges, they reminded the members of all they were called to be for one another.

---

4 J. Joseph Martos, *Doors to the Sacred* (Garden City, NY: Doubleday, 1982) p. 26.
5 K.W. Dillistone. *The Power of Symbol in Religion and Culture* (New York: Crossroads, 1986).

SYMBOL EXAMPLES

OVERVIEW

Good symbols need to be more than clever ideas. The symbols that have the best chance of enduring are those rooted in some of our ancient symbols, such as water, rainbows, wind. These symbols have maintained for centuries a meaning beyond their simple, concrete definitions. They possess the power to become the focal point of a group and a means by which the group can interpret its own actions. In struggling to find symbols for your group, keep in mind how the group understands itself, what ancient symbols are common to their understanding and their culture, the group's vision itself and how the symbol will relate to that vision.

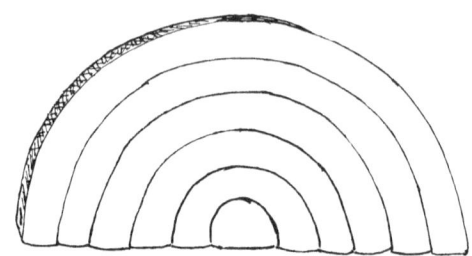

Rainbow

A rainbow can be made with an arc for each family. A center semi-circle allows for an eighth household, or a piece to represent the Church, the base on which we rest. Rainbows are a sign of covenant and hope.(Ritual: page 126)

SYMBOLS

The following symbols have been adapted and used in youth groups, intergenerational groups, and family faith formation groups with varying degrees of success. They are offered here not to be reproduced, but to jumpstart your own symbolic thinking and provide vehicles for the ritual actions that will be discussed later. In creating your symbol, make it beautiful und durable and deserving of respect.

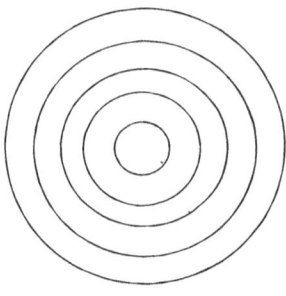

Concentric Circles

Concentric circles can be carved out of wood or cut out of heavy cardboard and given to families to decorate. The circle is a sign of eternity, of connection, of equality, of reality that never ends. (Ritual: page 129)

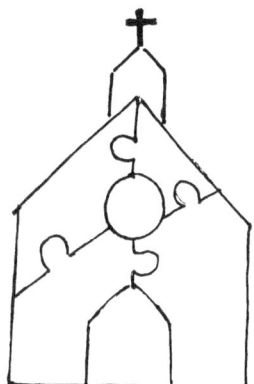

Church

A church can be made out of wood or heavy cardboard and cut into puzzle pieces, with a piece for each family, or members, and one piece to represent the rest of the community. The members decorate their piece. A small cross or crucifix for the top of the steeple can be carried home by the family member that will host the next meeting, or the member that will lead prayer, or the leader, or a designated "cross-bearer." (No specific ritual is given, but "The Cross" on page 128 can be used effectively)

Crosses

One of the most basic symbols of Christianity, crosses can be constructed in many ways. The beams of a wooden cross can represent the families/members and fit together, puzzle-style, when the families are assembled. A cross can be made from narrow logs, halved to lie flat, with hollows carved out for candles. Each family or member is given a candle to light up the cross. Square crosses can be constructed to fit together in a pattern that always seems incomplete and longs for more crosses. Crosses can be made of wood and decorated by families/members. (Ritual: page 128)

Star

A five-pointed Star, or star of David, carved out of wood or heavy cardboard, with a diamond for each family member. A five-pronged star can be made with a central circle. The star has represented a "way to Jesus" since the first Epiphany, as well as a guiding light to all navigators. (Ritual: page 131)

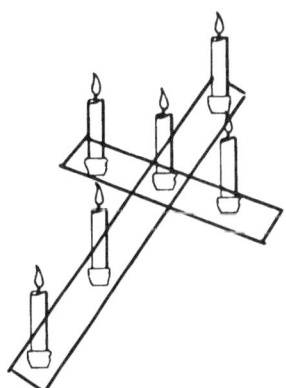

Fire

A central candle can be placed in a base that allows a candle for each family or member to be mounted around it. The opening ritual will include taking light from the central candle to light the individual ones. Sharing the light can also be demonstrated by using different-colored candles for the families/members and a central, large white one for the group. At the end of each meeting, families/members allow a little of the colored wax from their candles to drip onto the white one, as part of their closing prayer. Eventually, the "group" candle will be transformed. Small votive candles can also be used for each family, or member, and the light can be carefully carried in them from home (or at least from outside the meeting place) into the meeting, since we also bring the light with us as well as receive it. (Ritual: page 125)

Ship

A ship can be made with masts for each family or member. The ship is a symbol of voyage; we depend on one another to help us catch the wind in our sails. (Ritual: page 124)

Water

A central, clear receptacle, with a spout for pouring, is needed to represent the group. Each family or member has a small vial for carrying water, something worthy to carry a symbol of life, not an old pill or soda bottle. Each member brings its water to the meeting and adds it to the receptacle. The group vase is only full when all the families/members are present. As they leave, members take water back from the vase; only now it as been changed by mingling with the group. Water from the groups can be taken to large group celebrations at church, where it is blessed and the same process takes place. (Ritual: page 122)

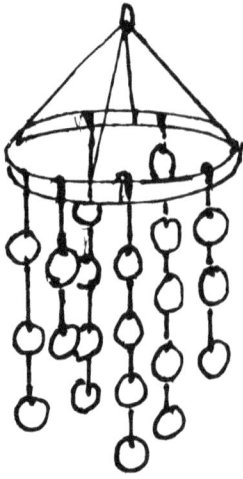

Wind Chimes

Wind chimes can be made from kits of shells created for that purpose. Each family is given a string of shells, one shell for each family member, which can be painted or decorated. A central circle represents the group, and the shells are hung from it each time the group gathers. The shells catch the music in the wind. The wind has been an accepted symbol of life and Spirit since early Hebrew Testament times. (Ritual: page 124)

Kite

A group can make and decorate a kite, perhaps use it for their covenant. Each family or member is given a "bow" to decorate for the tail. The kite reminds us again of the wind, the power of the spirit in our lives, while the tail reminds us of the balance we offer to each other. (Ritual: page 124)

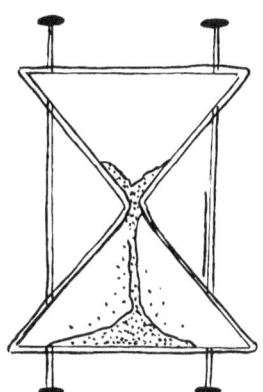

Minute Timers

Egg timers and one-minute timers are available from most kitchen supply stores. They can be brought to each meeting as a symbol of the time we are willing to give to God and to each other. (Ritual: page 127)

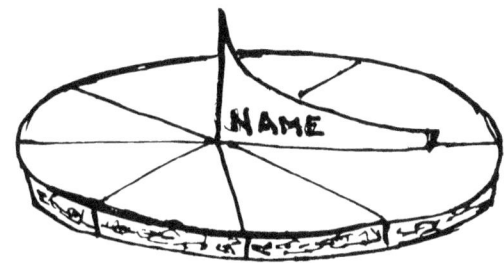

Sundial

A sundial can be constructed of wood or heavy card-board in pieces that can be covered with foil mottled to look like weathered metal, and given to each family or member. Sundials remind us not only of the significance of time, but the significance of shadows in helping us to understand the "time" in our life. Sundials remind us where the sun is when all we can see are shadows. (Ritual: page 127)

A COMMUNITY CELEBRATES RITUALS

"Ritual is the means by which collective beliefs and ideals are simultaneously generated, experienced, and affirmed as real by the community."[6] *Aidan Cavanaugh calls it the way we revlew and renew what we believe.*

Ritual offers us the opportunity to pray in a comfortable, known fashion. Just as practice exercises on the piano strengthen specific fingers and muscles by repetition, ritual is the opportunity to "practice" praying, a familiar gateway to a prayerful mindset. Its very familiarity is part of its great value. And just as the piano exercises can be beautiful music (check out J.S. Bach), so simple rituals can also comprise beautiful prayer.

The following rituals are offered with this in mind. They follow the same general format, and the same ritual can be used repeatedly by a group. Those in this section offer the opportunity to celebrate specific times, places, and ideas with ritual. Those in the next section are created around the symbols suggested on the previous pages for group use. All of the rituals can be used by any group simply by using the adaptations recommended in each "preparation" section. Directions for assembling a group symbol are included in italics wherever this is appropriate. A simple closing given with many of the rituals offers the opportunity to send households or individuals home at the end of the meeting with their piece of the symbol.

All of the rituals are designed as simple introductions to group meetings or classes. They can be developed into longer rituals that stand alone by using the possible readings included at the end of each ritual and by closing with the Lord's Prayer and song.

---

6 Emile Durkeim. *The Elementary Forms of Religious Life.* trans. J.W. Swain (New York: Free Press, 1965) p. 51.

QUESTIONING

PREPARATION

Instruct each person to choose a question from Scripture. A list of possible questions is included here, but encourage people to look for their own. Ask families to help little ones by reading several questions and talking about their possible meanings. Once each person in the household has chosen a question, ask him/her to choose one that represents the feelings of the family as a whole. It may be one of the ones an individual chose, or a totally different question.

List of Possible Questions

- Am I my brother's keeper? (Gen. 4:9)
- I lift my eyes to the mountains; from where shall come my help? (Ps. 121:1)
- Where can I hide from your Spirit? (Ps. 139:7)
- Who do you say that I am? (Matt. 16:14)
- Who are you, Lord? (Acts 9:5)
- What sign will you give to show us that we should believe in you? (John 6:30)
- How can a grown person be born again? Can we go back into our mother's womb and be born again? (John 3:4-5)
- Are you "He who is to come" or do we look for another? (Matt. 11:4)
- Is it lawful to work a cure on the Sabbath? (Matt. 12:10)
- What is truth? (John 18:38)
- Who is the greatest in the kingdom of heaven? (Matt. 18:1)
- What about us? .. . We have left everything and followed you. (Mark 10:28)
- How can anyone give this people sufficient bread? (Mark 8:4)
- Have (we) eyes, but no sight; ears but no hearing? (Mark 17:18)
- Good Teacher, what must I do to have everlasting life? (Mark 10:17)
- What do you want me to do for you? (Matt. 20:32)
- How long will you hide your face from me? (Ps. 18:2)
- How can this be? (Luke 1:34)

Parents may want to help children remember their quote by writing out the question and letting them carry it to the meeting.

RITUAL

Opening Song: Choose any song that focuses on searching, on our uncertainty.

Leader: We are so uncertain, God.

    We long for answers.

    We want to be sure.

    Sure that we have followed the right path,

    Certain we have spoken the right words.

    Studied the right chapters,

    Chosen the right friends.

    Help us to remember that You are mystery, Life is mystery.

    Help us to live with the questions.

In groups using symbol as an expression of unity, households come forward, one at a time, add their piece of the symbol, and speak their *family* question.

    (Allow the group to sit quietly for a few moments, then the leader voices her question aloud. Other people speak up randomly until all questions have been shared.)

Leader: Help us to remember, Lord,
    that You are mystery.

    Help us to live with the questions,

    One day at a time,

    One word at a time.

    You commanded us to ask for our needs, and so I invite each of us to voice our special intentions. We will respond, "Hear us, O Lord."

    (Spontaneous prayer of the faithful)

Leader: We ask that you hear us, Lord,
    and answer our needs.
    We ask this in the name of Jesus.

(Depending on what is to follow, you may want to repeat your opening song, a group theme song, or move directly to the next part of the meeting.)

CLOSING

Leader: Questions are starting points,

    Beginnings of new journeys,

    Windows

    To insight

    And deeper faith.

Invite each of the families/households to come forward and take their piece of the symbol, while saying: "Lord, keep our family open to all the questions in our lives."

    Because the questions themselves are Scripture, no additional readings are given for this ritual.

BREAD

PREPARATION

The leader should prepare a centerpiece around the theme of bread, with a special plate holding an unconsecrated host in the center. Ask each family/household or individual to bring a particular type of bread to the meeting. It is okay to buy the bread, but better not to have it sliced and packaged. Assign different types of bread to different families or individuals. You will need whole wheat or a basic yeast bread, soda bread, unleavened bread (such as matza), crackers, gingerbread. Ask everyone to bring the bread in a low basket with a linen napkin. Ask the family/household to designate someone who will hold it aloft while the prayer over it is being spoken, then add it to the centerpiece of bread.

RITUAL

Opening Song: "I Am the Bread of Life," or any song that focuses on bread-of-life themes.

Reader 1: "I am the bread of life.

Whoever comes to me will never be hungry; and those who believe in me will never thirst." John 6:35

Reader 2: Lord, *(Basic bread held up by member)*

We, too, are bread
   for the life of the world.

But there are many kinds of bread.

As there are many people.

There is the ordinary
   yeast (whole wheat) bread,

Breads that have been given
   ample time and warmth
   for the yeast to grow,

Families favored
   with stable homes,
   enough to eat.

May we use their gifts
   to nourish the world.

(soda bread held aloft by member)

> There is soda bread,
>> quick bread;
>
> Those who are in need,
>> who have no time to wait
>> for yeast to rise.
>
> Our bread has raisins,
>> for though they are wanting
>> they are still gifted
>> and still deserving
>> of the good things of the earth.
>
> May we remember their need
>> as we nourish the earth.

(unleavened bread raised)

> Unleavened bread
>> is for those
>> who have been flattened
>> by oppression and injustice.
>
> Let our hunger for bread
>> teach us to hunger and thirst
>> for justice.

(crackers raised)

> Crackers
>> represent the elderly,
>> salty with wisdom,
>> fragile with age.
>
> Let this bread
>> teach us to value wisdom,
>> to treat it gently
>
> When it has grown fragile.

(Gingerbread raised)

> Gingerbread,
>> spicy bread,
>> for all those
>> who do more than nourish,
>> who bring spice to our lives.

(Leader raises unconsecrated host.)

Leader: "Blessed are you, Lord,
God of all creation.
Through your goodness
we have this bread to offer,
which earth has given
and human hands
(Leader raises unconsecrated host.)
have made.
It will become for us
the bread of life."

Leader: Think for a moment of the people
who have been bread in your life.
We will pass each loaf of bread.
Break a piece and pray for
someone you have known
who has been gingerbread,
whole wheat bread, etc.

(Play quiet music until everyone has had a chance to have a small piece of each bread.)

Leader: Help us to remember, Lord,
we are called to be bread for the world.
We ask this in the name of Jesus.

All: Amen.

BEAUTY OF AUTUMN

(For areas where leaves change color)

PREPARATION

Ask each family or household to go for a walk. Each person is to find a leaf which, for some reason, reminds her of herself, then prepare a one-line prayer, thanking God for the particular trait that she and the leaf share, e.g., "Thank you, God, for making me solid and dependable like the stem of the hickory leaf."

RITUAL

Opening Song: Any song that deals with the beauty of creation, any thanksgiving song.

Reader 1: "We are God's work of art,
 created in Christ Jesus
 to live the good life
 as from the beginning
 he meant us to live it." *(Ephesians 2:10)*

Reader 2: God, our God,

 You have painted our world.

 Had You given us
  just one maple,
  one tree that changed
  magnificently with the seasons,
  we would have been in awe.

 We would have fenced it round,
  named it
  one of the seven wonders
   of the world,
  and planned to visit
  at least once in our lifetime.

 But You lavish us with beauty
  and, glutted,
  we risk walking unseeing
  through Your world.

 Open our eyes
  to the beauty of our world
  and each other.

Leader: *(Placing the leaf in a vase and placing first piece of family symbol)*
"Thank you, God, for making me… ."

(Other individuals follow, families or households placing their symbol as each person from that household comes forward with a leaf.)

Leader: Loving God,
 the earth is beautiful in its dying.

 Let it remind us of the power that pain and death have to make us beautiful.

 We ask this in the name of Jesus.

All: Amen.

Possible Readings

Ephesians 2:1-10, Isaiah 43:1-2

BEGINNING OF THE SCHOOL YEAR

PREPARATION

Have each person bring a symbol of school opening. Make a small centerpiece of books, pencils, calculator and candle, with space for group members to add their own symbols *and to assemble the group symbol*. Parents may want to bring symbols of making lunches or carpooling; singles may be taking a course, or bring a symbol of driving more carefully or leaving earlier to allow for school buses.

RITUAL

Opening Song: Since it is likely that this will be your first meeting of the year, simply choose an upbeat, gathering song.

Reader 1: "Now, Lord, give me wisdom and knowledge." *(2 Chr. 1:12)*

Reader 2: Learning,
for some of us, so easy,
so filled with rewards,

For others, so difficult,
so filled with frustration.

Help us, God, to be patient
with our own limits
and with the limits of others,

To give one another
the space and time
each needs to grow.

(The leader explains that he will call each family forward with a prayer for them, and they can add their school symbol to the centerpiece. As they come forward, they may voice any specific prayers they have, and the group will respond, **Lord, hear our prayer.**)

Leader: May the N......... family/household
have a peace-filled
and productive school year.

(The household named comes forward, adds their school symbol to the centerpiece *and places their piece of the group symbol*. Encourage families to word their petitions as prayers, e.g., "For our Aunt Lucy, we pray to the Lord"; not "I want to pray for...")

Leader: Lord, our God,

You are the source of all knowledge

Keep us focused in our studies.

Help us to understand
that all study is a prayer
and part of the way
we seek you.

We ask this in the name of Jesus.

All: Amen.

CLOSING

Leader: (Invite each family to come forward as their names are called and take back their school symbol *and their piece of the group symbol*.)

Leader: God, Source of all wisdom,
bless the N...... family/household.

Help them to study with diligence
and work with patience
during the upcoming school year.

Closing Song

Opening song or song appropriate to the lesson.

WAITING (ADVENT)

PREPARATION

There is no "at home" preparation for this ritual, but the leader can help the group prepare by asking them to quiet down and think about what it feels like to wait. Think of one word to describe that feeling. During the prayer, the leader is going to say "Waiting feels like…" and each person will be free to speak her word aloud. Parents could help little ones think of a word that describes the feeling of waiting

RITUAL

Opening Song: Choose a gentle Advent song, like "Patience, People," from the St. Louis Jesuits' *Calm Is the Night* album. Invite the group to listen to it.

Reader 1: "More than the watchman waits for the dawn, my soul waits for the Lord." *(Psalm 130:6)*

Reader 2: All of us wait.

Each day brings its own dose
of waiting.

We wait
in dentists' offices,
at sports practices,
at school.

We wait for supper to be ready,
for the paper to be given back,
for the refund,
for the letter from a friend.

We wait
to be big enough
to ride the roller coaster,
old enough to stay up late,
secure enough to be on our own.

Our waiting feels like…. *(give people a chance to voice their feeling).*

Advent calls us to celebrate waiting.

Each time we wait,
help us to remember
how the world waited for a Savior.

Help us to remember
we are always waiting
for Your return.

Help us to find and recognize You
in each other

As we wait.

We are an Advent people.

Family/Household:
Lord, the N……. family is waiting for you. *(As each family speaks this phrase, they come forward and place their piece of the symbol.)*

All: Come, Lord Jesus.

Song: "Come, Lord Jesus" by Carey Landry, or other gentle Advent song.

Possible Readings

Habakkuk 2:2-3, Psalm 33:20-22, Psalm 130:5-6
Luke 2:26-38

WINTER

PREPARATION

This is a ritual for places that experience snow in winter. Ask families to think about what snow means to them and to bring a symbol of winter to the meeting. They may want to bring paper snowflakes, shovels, mittens, hats, etc. If you have an old coat tree, it would make an excellent centerpiece for this prayer.

RITUAL

Opening Song: Any winter song.

Reader 1: "You are the maker of day and night,
You instituted light and sun,
You fixed the boundaries of the world,
You created summer and winter."
(Psalm 74:16-17)

Reader 2: Winter,

The earth lies dormant,
the trees,
the seeds,
the animals.

Lie sleeping.

Long, dark nights,
dwindling daylight

Turn our thoughts homeward,
to lighted windows
and blazing hearths.

Snow blankets the earth
pretending
the world is pure—

And the children,
those who *are* pure,

slide on its surface
and delight in its newness.

Let the winter cold,
the treachery of ice,
the deceptiveness of snow
remind us to look homeward.

Leader: God of winter and summer,
help us to remember
that life is cyclical.

We need a dormant period
to bring forth fruit.

Teach us patience
as we wait for spring.

We ask this in the name of Jesus.

All: Amen.

(The leader explains that the group will present the articles they have brought to the meeting and each will be described as a reason to praise God. For example, someone may present mittens and say, "For mittens, which protect our hands from the cold…" and the group will respond, "We praise you, Lord." Each of the articles will be added to the centerpiece.)

Leader: Let every season become a reminder to praise you, O Lord.

Song: Repeat Opening song

THE DESERT (LENT)

PREPARATION

Ask each person to bring a rock to the meeting. If you are in an area that has no rocks, some sand. Ask each person to think of a fault they wish to give up for Lent. Some suggestions would be: busyness, not listening, impatience, anger, talking back, disrespect, unkindness, lying, etc. Prepare a centerpiece for prayer with a desert theme.

RITUAL

Opening Song: Any song with a Lenten, desert theme. "Come Back To Me" by Weston Priory, or something similar.

Reader 1: "The Spirit drove Jesus into the desert, and he remained there for forty days." *(Mark 1:12)*

Reader 2: Deserts
are empty places,

Hot and dry
in the glaring light of the sun,

Cold and desolate at night.

We are afraid of the desert.

We avoid the heat and the cold,
the loneliness,

But in the desert,
stripped of the distractions,
the incidentals that crowd our days,

We are free
to discover ourselves
and meet our God.

Leader: Lord, our hearts grow cold as stone,
dry as sand.

Here in the desert,
take away our stony hearts
and give us hearts of flesh.

(Leader surrenders stone or sand to centerpiece and prays:)

Leader: Lord, this Lent, I surrender (give up) .... which makes my heart stony.

(Each of the people adds a stone or sand to the centerpiece and states the fault they wish to give up for Lent. *When everyone has surrendered a stone, one person from each household comes forward with their piece of the symbol and places it, saying: "Lord, help us to be present to you and to each other this Lent."*)

Leader: Loving God, forgive our faults.

Take away our hearts of stone
and give us new hearts.

We ask this in the name of Jesus.

All: Amen.

Possible Readings

Ezekiel 36:24-29, Luke 4:1-13

DESERT (ALTERNATIVE)

PREPARATION

This ritual can be extended into an entire lesson by giving the members of the group the opportunity to make sand paintings at the end of the prayer. Colored sand can usually be purchased at craft stores, and the paintings can be made in clear plastic glasses or baby food jars and sealed with melted wax.

Begin by asking the group to sit quietly and think about the images the word "desert" conveys.

RITUAL

Opening Song: Any song that reflects on the desert experience.

Reader 1: "I will turn the desert into pools of water and the dry land into flowing springs." *(Isaiah 41:18)*

Reader 2: The desert.
>Empty,
>Barren,
>Lonely.

>What do you think of when you think of desert?

(Allow the members of the group to softly voice words that describe desert for them.)

>In times of plenty,
>>we forget about our need,
>>we forget about God.

>We need the desert to remind us,
>>to strip us bare
>>of all our distractions,

>To focus us once again
>>on our purpose,
>>our call,
>>Our God.

Leader: Jesus went to the desert to pray. It is important for each of us to create a quiet desert within, where we can be alone with God. It is the prayer of the desert that brings us back again to share with one another.

(*Members of the group come forward with their piece of the symbol, saying: "Help us to be present to God and to each other."*)

(If you are making sand paintings, begin playing quiet music, distribute materials and ask everyone to make a painting that reminds them of the prayerfulness of the desert.)

CLOSING

Leader: Often we are led
>into the desert,
>but sometimes
>we create our own desert

>By forgetting
>>to nurture our dreams
>>and feed our aspirations,

>By neglecting to drink deep
>>of the waters of life.

(Families/households come forward to accept their symbol.)

Leader: N..., create a desert space within you and water *it with prayer.*

Family/Household: *We will*

Song: "Come to the Water" or a similar song about quenching thirst.

Possible Readings

Isaiah 41:17-18, Isaiah 44:3-4, Luke 4:1-13

NEW LIFE (EASTER/SPRING)

PREPARATION

Ask families to take a walk and look for signs of new life in the world around them, bringing one sign to the meeting. The leader prepares a centerpiece with some signs of new life.

RITUAL

Opening Song: An Easter song.

Reader 1: "I am the resurrection and the life. All who believe in me, even if they die, will live forever." *(John 11:25)*

Reader 2: Winter has passed,
the earth struggles
to give birth.

Prepared by the barrenness,
made fertile
by lying fallow,

The earth is ready.

We, too, have prepared
in silence,
in solitude,
in the Lenten desert.

May our preparation
bring forth much fruit.

Leader: God of life,
You promised us new life
in and through Your Son.

Open our hearts and alert our minds
to the signs of that life.

(Leader calls forth one family/household/member at a time. All add their sign of new life to the centerpiece *and their pieces of the symbol to the group symbol*, while saying)

Member: Open our eyes, Lord,
to all the life You are calling forth
in each of us.

All: Amen.

Leader: God of life,
help us to celebrate this Easter season with joy,
knowing that beyond every death
there is new life

All: Amen.

Song: Any Easter Song

Possible Readings:

Luke 24:13-35, John 21:1-23 or any of the Resurrection narratives.

SUMMER VACATION

PREPARATION

Ask each member to bring a symbol of vacation time. Family members may each want to bring an individual symbol. The leader should prepare a centerpiece with symbols of the school year.

RITUAL

Opening Song: A song that deals with new life or rest.

Reader 1: "Send forth your Spirit, Lord, and we shall be recreated."

Reader 2: Vacation,
Summer,
A time for recreation,
A time to be re-created.
A time to play.
A time to rest.
A time for empty space
In the crowded rush
of our lives.
A time
for being renewed.

Leader: God who makes all things new,
renew us through this vacation time.

Rest our bodies and our spirits
so that we may begin again,
refreshed and renewed

Many of us have worked hard in school,
helping children in school,
carpooling to sports,

But our efforts are off-balance
without time to be refreshed.

(Leader begins to change centerpiece by adding his symbol for vacation and saying:)

Leader: Thank you, God for……

(Each of the members of the group do the same, adding symbols as they thank God for something specific about summer which the symbol represents. *If the group is assembling a symbol, this is done at the same time.*)

Leader: Let us pray for our special needs over the coming months.

(Spontaneous prayer of the faithful, to which the group responds, Lord, hear our prayer.)

Leader: Protect us, God of refreshment, throughout our vacation time, and let us never forget You. We ask this in the name of Jesus.

All: Amen.

Possible Reading

Matthew 11:28-30

A COMMUNITY'S RITUALS ARE ROOTED IN SYMBOLS

*The following rituals were designed specifically for use with the symbols given earlier in this book. The page where a specific symbol can be found is listed with each ritual. The rituals are not **limited** to this use only, however. Other groups of individuals, as well as intergenerational groups, will find the ritual adaptations simple and easy to follow. Groups using one symbol may choose a different ritual to awaken the community, stress a certain time of year or need in the group, or simply because they like a particular ritual.*

WATER

PREPARATION

This ritual was written to be used by those groups who use water as their symbol (see page 104). It can be used by others simply by asking each household (or individual) to bring a small vial or bottle of water from their own home to the meeting. The leader prepares a centerpiece with a Bible, a candle, and a large clear container from which water can be easily poured.

RITUAL

Opening Song: Any song that deals with water, coming together, etc.

(Lower lights)

Reader 1: "In the beginning, God created the heavens and the earth. Now the earth was a formless void, there was darkness over the deep, and God's Spirit hovered over the water." *(Genesis 1:1-2)*

Reader 2: Water,
> Symbol of life.

> We are born of water,
>> in birth and baptism,
>> we bless ourselves,
>> bathe ourselves,
>> refresh ourselves,
>>> in water.

> We stand awestruck before the ocean,
>> powerless before the flood,
>> breathless before the waterfall,

> As water reminds us
>> of the awesome presence of God.

(Leader invites members of each household to reverently hold up the water they have brought.)

Leader: Lord,
> you brought forth water from the rock,

> You parted the sea
>> and calmed the storm.

> Bless this water now,
>> symbol of our very selves.

> Let it mingle with the water of others
>> and bring forth new life.

(Each family/household/individual comes forward and pours water into the large container, saying the following prayer while pouring:)

Family: We, the N........, commit ourselves and our gifts to the life of the community. We pray especially today for...
(any personal need may be mentioned).

All: Lord, hear our prayer.

Leader: Lord, make us one
> as the water in this vial has become
> one. Keep us attentive to You
> and to one another,
> and may this sharing
> bring forth new life.

All: Amen.

CLOSING

(The leader invites the group to reflect on the evening they have just shared, then calls each family forward, one by one, and refills their small vial while saying:)

Leader: N......, receive this water,
symbol of your life in Christ,
changed by the water
with which it has mingled,
by the community and the lives
you have shared.

Treasure the water
as you treasure your community.

Family: Amen.

Closing Song: Joyful, focus on water, baptism, community

Possible Readings:

Jeremiah 17:7-8, Isaiah 55:1-3, Isaiah 55:8-11, Isaiah 49:8-11, John 4:13-14, Isaiah 44:3-5

WIND

PREPARATION

This ritual was designed to be used by a group that has chosen to use the kite or wind chimes as its symbol. It can be used effectively in other groups by preparing people in advance. Each household (individual) makes a ribbon to be tied on the tail of the kite with their name and the gifts (done in pictures or words) which they feel they bring to the community. The leader needs to provide a kite, with a long tail for attaching the ribbon ties. Or the leader can provide a basic ring, and each household can be given a string of chimes (see page 104) with a chime decorated for each person. (This prayer service can also provide an opening ritual for those who use a ship and sails for their symbol, page 104.)

RITUAL

Opening Song: A song of the Spirit that speaks of the Spirit as wind or breath. "Wind Beneath My Wings" by Bette Midler is very appropriate, if you have access to it.

Reader 1: "Yahweh drove back the sea with a strong wind, and made the dry land appear." *(Exodus 14:22)*

Reader 2: Wind,
> sometimes howling
> across the earth,
> shaking the very mountains
> with its power,

> Sometimes moving gently,
> caressing the treetops,
> ruffling the waters
> as it whispers by.

> We lift sails,
> erect windmills,
> hang wind chimes
> in calculated attempts
> to tap into
> its awesome power.

> But we cannot harness the wind,
> we cannot capture or contain it.

> Like the Spirit,
> it blows where it will.

(Invite each family to come forward to add their tie to the Kite or their chimes to the wind chime ring.)

Family: Spirit-God, touch the N..... family and keep us attentive to Your touch and to one another. We pray especially for...

All: Hear us, O God.

Leader: Spirit-God, You blow where You will, giving power to our movement and music to our lives.

> Open us up to be always aware of Your presence and willing and able to respond. We ask this in the name of Jesus.

All: Amen.

CLOSING

(Leader calls each family or household forward, presenting them with their portion of the symbol.)

Leader: May the Spirit of God be present in the N.... family, as a powerful wind filling you with strength, a gentle breath, filling you with life.

All: Amen.

Possible Readings

John 3:7-8, 1 Kings 18:45, Acts 2:1-4

FIRE

PREPARATION

This ritual was prepared for those who use candles as symbols for their group (see page 103). However, it can be used successfully with another group simply by inviting each household (or individual) to bring a candle to the group or by providing one. The leader prepares a centerpiece in which a candle figures prominently as the focus for the prayer, with a candle holder for each of the candles members will be bringing.

RITUAL

Opening Song: The opening song needs to focus on light. Anything from the camp song, "I've Got A Light," to something about Christ, the Light of the World, will work well. Lights are then extinguished. Reader 1 may read with a small flashlight.

Reader 1: "The people that walked in darkness / Have seen a great light. / On those who live in a land of deep shadow / A light has shown." *(Isaiah 9:1)*

(The leader lights the central candle.)

Reader 2: Fire,
> our physical assault
> on the darkness.

> No longer must we wait for the dawn,
> for we are capable
> of bringing light
> into this darkness.

> Fire,
> our commitment
> to challenge the darkness
> that threatens to envelop us,

> For no amount of darkness
> can overcome
> our one, small flame.

(Leader calls each household/individual forward, one at a time, to light their candle and place it with the central candle. Each person/family recites while doing this:)

Family: Help us, Lord,
> to let your light shine within us
> and give light to others.

> Let your light shine especially on…
> (Household mentions any particular prayers).

All: God of Light, hear us.

Leader: Light a fire in our hearts, Lord,
> capable of consuming
> and transforming the earth.

> We ask this in the name of Jesus.

All: Amen.

CLOSING

(The leader calls each of the families forward, one at a time, and hands each a lighted candle.)

Leader: N....., the light is within you.

(Family blows out the candle.)

Possible Readings

John 1:1-5, Isaiah 9:1-4

RAINBOWS

PREPARATION

This ritual is most effectively celebrated outside, in daylight. When this is the case, have every household/individual bring "bubble stuff" and a wand. It can be done effectively inside by creating an arc of the rainbow for each household (see page 102).

RITUAL

Opening Song: Any rainbow song.

Reader 1: "God said, 'Here is the sign of the Covenant I make between Myself and you and every living creature with you for all generations: I set my bow in the clouds and it shall be a sign of the Covenant between Me and the earth.'" *(Genesis 9:12-13)*

Reader 2: Rainbows,
God's promise to the earth.

God, Who is light,
has passed through our existence,
bending to us

To reveal the colors,
the beauty
of divine love.

We, too, are called
to be rainbows for others,
refracting the divine,
revealing the colors of God's love,
as the light passes through us.

(If the ritual takes place outside, the leader makes a bubble with the wand and says softly as it rises:)

Leader: Help me to be a rainbow for others.

(Leader invites group members to do the same.)

(If the ritual takes place inside, each family/household comes forward, placing their arc in the rainbow and saying:)

Family: God, help us to be present to each other this evening, so that together we may fully reflect the beauty of your love.

All: Amen.

Leader: You have called us Lord,
to be a rainbow people, filled with light,
reflecting Your love.

May our time together
create rainbows in each of our hearts.

We ask this in the name of Jesus.

All: Amen.

CLOSING

Leader: N..., be true to the color God calls you to be and carry the rainbow of God's promise in your heart.

(While saying these words, the leader hands each household/family/individual their arc.)

Possible Readings

Genesis 9:12-16, Revelations 4:1-3

TIME

PREPARATION

This prayer service can be used with the sundial symbol or a leader can have each household/individual bring a small amount of sand in a little glass jar. (Baby food jars work well.) The leader supplies a fairly large vase with a small opening and a funnel, clear if possible. (This will make a makeshift hourglass. The opening in the funnel can be made smaller by putting tape around the inside. Make sure there is no stickiness on the outside of the tape, since this could cause the funnel to clog.) The leader makes a centerpiece around the makeshift hourglass or the central piece of the sundial. (Also, see page 105.)

RITUAL

Opening Song: Any song that focuses on "time": "A Time Will Come For Singing," from the St. Louis Jesuits, "For Everything A Season," etc.

Reader 1: "There is a season for everything, a time for every occupation under heaven." *(Ecc. 3:1)*

Reader 2: Time,
    it marks its quiet passage
    through our days and nights.

We speak of "having" it,
    "saving" it, "spending" it,
    "using" it or "wasting" it,

Perhaps, even "giving" it.

But it is all illusion;
    it was never ours.

It slips through our lives
    as sand through the hourglass,
    as sun across the sky.

We have only the moment,
    the Now,
    the time in which to build
        the timeless eternal.

Leader: Eternal God, we place the time,
our past and our future, in Your hands.
Help us to be present in the Now,
to fill each moment with Your love,
one moment at a time.

(Leader pours sand into makeshift hourglass or adds piece to the sundial.)

Leader: I relinquish my attempt to control time and ask You, God, to help me to be truly present to You, to others, and especially to ... (mentions any Special need).

All: Listen to our prayer.

(Each family/household repeats the action. If you have very young children in the group, change the word "relinquish" to "let go of." Children do not attempt to control time anyway, but that is a very big word for them.)

CLOSING

The leader gives each family/individual their piece of the sundial or pours sand back into their jar, saying:

Leader: N..., receive this time as a gift. Give yourselves fully to each moment and to everything that touches your lives.

All: Amen.

Possible Readings

Ecclesiastes 3:1-8, Mark 1:14-15, Matthew 6:25-34, John 9:4-5

THE CROSS

PREPARATION

This ritual can be used with any of the symbols based on the cross (see page 103), or without any group symbol. It can be very unifying for a group to present all of the members with small wooden crosses to be worn as a symbol of their Christian faith and their commitment to the community. A ritual for presenting crosses is given as the closing of this particular prayer.

RITUAL

Opening Song: Although the symbol of this ritual is the cross, the theme is really following Jesus. "I Have Decided to Follow Jesus" or any song that emphasizes following Jesus will work well.

Reader 1: "If any of you want to be a follower of mine, you must renounce yourself and take up your cross and follow me." *(Mark 8:34)*

Reader 2: Three crosses
    standing empty on a hill,
    not just a sign
    of suffering and death,

But of new life.

Their beams stretch upward
    toward heaven,
    outward
    toward earth,

A stark reminder
    that suffering calls us
    to reach upward
    (or downward)

Toward God,
    and outward
    toward each other,

That our pain
    might also lead
    to new life.

Leader: God of goodness, we are bound together in our weakness, bonded by our pain. Help us always to reach out to one another. (Adding his piece of the cross symbol, the leader says:)

Help me to be aware of the needs of my community and my world, particularly the needs of… (leader prays for personal intentions; group responds: "**Hear us, O God.**")

(Each household/individual adds piece to the symbol. If the group is not using a symbol, a simple prayer of the faithful can be added here, with particular attention to those who are suffering.)

Leader: Help us, O God of the weak,
    as we take up our cross to follow You.

All: Amen.

CLOSING

Leader: N…, receive this cross (piece of the cross, candle from the cross) as a sign of your commitment to Christ, your community and the world.

All: Amen.

Possible Readings

Mark 8:34-36, Luke 9:23-26, Isaiah 43:1-3

CIRCLES

PREPARATION

This ritual was designed to be used with groups using concentric circles as a symbol (see page 102). This symbol can be created for the meeting by making the circles in advance out of cardboard, giving each member (family) a circle, and asking them to prepare by decorating it for the next meeting. The ritual can also be done without the symbol.

You may want to begin by asking a child to demonstrate the motion of the earth. Once he is standing and spinning, ask another child to be the sun. Direct your spinning earth to travel around the sun. Ask the sun to begin to travel around the room with the earth still spinning circles around it. The group can then imagine the room spinning on its own orbit. This gives a graphic picture of the circles of our universe.

RITUAL

Opening Song: The theme of this prayer is both unity and eternity. Any song that focuses on one of these themes will work. Have everyone join hands in a circle for the song. (Keep the song simple so that members don't need to be holding words.)

Reader 1: "God, who lives above the circle that is the earth … has stretched out the heavens like a cloth, spread them like a tent for humanity to live in." *(Isaiah 40:22)*

Reader 2: We live on a spinning circle,
    traveling in circles around the sun,
    in a solar system
        that circles within a galaxy,
    in a galaxy that circles in a universe.

The circle,
    no beginning,
    no end,

A constant reminder
    of the eternity of God.

Circular motion,
    finding the source of its energy
    in the center,

A constant reminder
    of our own needs.

We are connected within that circle.

Dependent on one another
    to be complete,
    to present the true image of God.

Leader: God of no beginning and end,
source of our strength and our motion,
help us to be connected to You
and to one another.

We ask this in the name of Jesus.

All: Amen.

(If the group is assembling a symbol, each family/household would come forward, one at a time, add their piece to the symbol and say:)

Member: We, the N… family, are a circle within circles, dependent on God and on one another for our strength. Tonight, Lord, we especially pray… (mentions any special need).

All: Lord, hear our prayer.

Leader: God of no beginning and end,
hear and answer the prayers of those united in the circle of Your love.

CLOSING

Leader presents each household with a piece of the circle, saying:

Leader: N.......family, let this circle remind you of your Center and your community.

All: Amen.

Possible Readings

John 14:1-4, 1 John 1-4

STARS

PREPARATION

There is no preparation to be done at home for this lesson. If you are assembling a star, members need to bring their pieces (see page 103). Whether or not you are using a symbol, you may want to begin by asking the group what they think of when they think of a star. If this ritual will be repeated each time the group meets, ask them to come back each time with a different idea of "star."

RITUAL

Opening Song: Any song that deals with stars, any kind, or a song about light.

Reader 1: "We have seen His star in the East and have come to adore the Lord." *(Matt. 2:2)*

Reader 2: It was a sign,
    and only the wise ones
      recognized it.

Have we seen His star?

Are we willing to set aside
    our lives,
    our wealth,
    our own "stardom"
      to follow His star?

Have we seen it in the East?

Leader: God,

Who placed the stars in the heavens
    and chose one
      to alert us to the birth of Your Son,

grant us the wisdom always
    to watch for Your signs.

Help us to respond with our gifts.

We ask this in the name of Jesus.

All: Amen.

(Each of the members or households comes forward one at a time and assembles the star, saying:)

Member: We, the N......family,
    will always try to follow Your star.

CLOSING

Leader calls each family forward, presents them with their piece of the symbol and says:

Leader: N..., carry the light of Christ in your hearts.

Song: (Any light song)

A COMMUNITY CELEBRATES PRAYER

The prayer services in this section of the book are designed to be done in conjunction with any of the family activities found earlier in this resource, as part of family retreats or workshops, or simply as prayer celebrations for families.

CELEBRATION OF MERCY

OVERVIEW

This is a ritual of forgiveness outside the sacrament of reconciliation. Its purpose is not only to seek God's forgiveness for ourselves, but to ask God to help us to forgive those who have hurt us. It is appropriate for Lent or Advent, or during family preparation for the reception of any of the sacraments. It is recommended in conjunction with "Lenten Crosses," for parishes looking for a more formal ending to that activity.

MATERIALS

- Small table
- Small linen cloth
- Large punch bowl
- Sugar cubes, enough for each person to have one
- Two pretty glass dishes
- Recording of reflective music

REMOTE PREPARATION

1. Read the "Reflection" part of this prayer service carefully. If you do not feel comfortable leading it, ask someone from the community whom you consider a good homilist. It is important *not to read* this section, but to reflect on the Scripture yourself and share it as a personal reflection on forgiveness. Any personal story you have about difficulty in forgiving would be very appropriate in this reflection.

2. Put the small table in the center of the room or church in which the ritual will be celebrated. Cover it with a small linen cloth.

3. Put the sugar cubes into the two small dishes, and place them on the table.

4. Prepare someone to do the reading and someone to lead the litany.

5. You may want to make up folders of the prayer service, with the invitation to prayer, the litany, and the responses. This is not necessary.

6. Just before you are to begin the ritual, fill the punch bowl with very warm water. It is important that the water be warm because you want the sugar to dissolve easily.

PRAYER EXPERIENCE

1. Opening Song: "River of Glory" by Dan Schutte or any song that relates forgiveness and water.

2. Call to Prayer:
   "God of the Prodigal…
   God of the elder son…
   God of Mary the virgin mother…
   God of Mary the Magdalene…
   God of the woman caught in adultery…
   God of those who would stone her…
   God of the Samaritan woman…
   God of the tax collector…
   God of the righteous…
   God of the sinner… We come to you.
   Elder sons and prodigals…
   Virgins and prostitutes…
   Just ones and sinners…
   Knowing ourselves as one of these…
   Knowing ourselves as all of these…
   we come before you,
   asking your forgiveness for our sins…
   asking you to fill us with your forgiveness
   for those who have sinned against us."

3. Prayer:
   "Loving and merciful God,
   we come before you,
   knowing that we are sinners,
   and seeking your mercy.
   You promise to forgive us
   as we forgive others.
   That is a hard saying, Lord.
   How often must I forgive?
   As often as you forgive me?
   Grant us your forgiveness,
   Lord and help us to forgive others."

   Response:
   "Lord, Jesus Christ, Son of the living God,
   have mercy on me, a sinner."

4. Litany:
   Response: Forgive us, O Lord.

   Leader:

   a. "For the times I have been less than honest, in my words and in my actions, with others, and with myself." R.

   b. "For those who have failed to be honest with me in what they said to me or what they said about me." R.

   c. "For the times my thoughtless words and actions have wounded others, for those whose words and actions have wounded me." R.

   d. "For the times I have been unfaithful to the promises I have made and for those who have been unfaithful to me." R.

   e. "For the times I let anger, rage and resentment rule my actions, and for those who have wounded me with their angry actions." R.

   f. "For my lack of compassion with the pain of others, and for those who failed to be compassionate with me." R.

   g. "For my inability to listen to others, and for all who refuse to listen to me." R.

   h. "For my rash judgments against others, and for others who judge me harshly." R.

   i. "For my preoccupation, with myself and my own activities, that keeps me from being truly present to you, and to others and even to myself." R.

5. Reading: Matthew 18:21-22

6. Reflection: "**What do you think it means, to forgive someone seventy times seven times?**" Invite the group to speak with each other. "**It certainly could mean that we are meant to forgive someone no matter how many times they hurt us. But there is another meaning here. Sometimes we have to forgive the same hurt over and over again. Do you ever find that, just when you think you have forgiven someone, the same hurt bubbles to the surface all over again, and you could get just as angry as you were the first time? Is it, sometimes, just not possible to forgive?**"

   "**Do you remember the story of the Prodigal Son? Who was it in that story that found it hard to forgive?**"

   By way of a response, give the group a chance to recap the story a little in case there is someone who does not know it.

   "**We may think we would have been willing to forgive, but don't forget, as the elder brother, you are the one who stayed home, you took on all your brother's work, you tried to support your father and comfort your mother, you listened to her crying and watched your father walking the roads. You have good reason to be angry. Let's look at what the father says.**"

7. Reading 2: Luke 15:25-32

8. Reflection: "**When the father said 'All that I have is yours,' I don't think he was talking about the farm or his money. I think he was talking about his forgiveness. When we just can't forgive, God invites us to accept his mercy, to simply give our hurt over and let him take care of it. That's what you are invited to do here today.**"

9. Presider walks to bowl in center and lifts water out with hands, letting it fall through into the bowl while saying:

   "**Lord God, Maker of the universe, bless this water. Let it become for all of us a sign of your great mercy.**"

   Presider lifts bowl of sugar cubes and says: "**Lord God, Maker of the Universe, bless these sugar cubes. Let them become for each of us a sign of the hurts we cannot forgive. Help us to name them, and to release them into your mercy—that you might do for us what we are unable to do for ourselves.**"

10. Invite each to come forward, whenever they are ready, and take a sugar cube. "**Name the cube after some hurt you have not been able to forgive, then surrender it to God's mercy by placing it in the water. Because we are called to take on the work of redemption, bless yourself with the water, taking on the hurts of all the people of your community.**"

11. Play soft music until all have returned to their seats. If the community is large, you may need tables with bowls of water and sugar in several locations.

12. Presider: "**Let us turn to one another with a sign of God's peace.**"

13. Close by singing "Prayer of St. Francis" by Sebastian Temple.

HOLY SPIRIT PRAYER

OVERVIEW

This prayer is designed to be celebrated by families during Pentecost, in preparation for confirmation, at the beginning or end of a confirmation retreat, or whenever a prayer service of the Spirit seems particularly appropriate. It could be done in conjunction with the activity on kites or on wind chimes.

MATERIALS

- Bubbles, a bottle for each family and one for the leader
- Bible
- Gifts of the Spirit, enough that each person present will get one
- Music for "Spirit, Come" by Gregory Norbert

REMOTE PREPARATION

1. Write the gifts of the Spirit out on symbols used to represent the Holy Spirit. (We used doves, flames, and bubbles.) Place these in baskets on a center table or altar.

2. Place a small bottle of soap bubbles, the kind that comes with a wand, on the table.

EXPERIENCE

1. Opening song: "Come Holy Ghost"

2. Invitation to Prayer (the leader blows bubbles slowly into the air while reading):
   **"If God is light…and the Spirit is breath…
   then we are the soap film…
   fragile, flat, transparent.
   Until we are filled with the Spirit…
   it is our task…filled with the Spirit…
   to bend the light…so that the light becomes rainbows. And all who have eyes to see…look upon us…and know what it is…to see God."**

3. Reading: Isaiah 61:1

4. Response: "Spirit, Come" by Gregory Norbert. As the song is sung, pass the basket with the gifts of the Spirit around, and invite everyone to take one. As you begin the prayer for the gifts, ask every person to join in reading the response to the gift that he or she has received. Parents should help little ones:

   L. "Spirit of Wisdom…"
   R. **"Awaken me."**

   L. "Spirit of Understanding…"
   R. **"Enlighten me."**

   L. "Spirit of Counsel…"
   R. **"Empower me."**

   L. "Spirit of Knowledge…"
   R. **"Inform me."**

   L. "Spirit of Courage…"
   R. **"Strengthen me."**

   L. "Spirit of Prayerfulness…"
   R. **"Sanctify me."**

   L. "Spirit of Reverence…"
   R. **"Overshadow me."**

5. All: **"Holy Spirit, you have filled the hearts of your faithful and enkindled in us the fire of your love. Recreate us and, through us, renew the face of the earth. Amen."**

6. As a closing song, use one of the Beatitude songs that the community knows, such as "Lead Me, Lord" by John D. Becker.

7. As the families are leaving, present each with a small container of bubbles saying: **"Go in the peace of the Spirit and renew the earth."**

A COMMUNITY COVENANTS TOGETHER

A covenant process can be used by any group or class of youth or adults that hopes to become a community. The Covenant services are appropriate for commissioning teachers and commitment ceremonies for opening classes and beginning small group studies.

Signing a covenant with all the members of a religious education class can be part of a commissioning ceremony for the teachers, and held during class time. It is necessary for the group to meet first with one another to write up their "contract," or covenant. It should contain the main points each person in the group thinks are necessary for the group to grow as a community. These things may be as straightforward as attending faithfully, and as complex as praying for one another and being aware of the needs of one another. Once a covenant is made, all the groups who have entered into the process meet at the church for a formal blessing and signing.

The principal celebrant for a covenant service does not need to be a priest or minister, but having the pastor will help to center the group more deeply in the life of the community.

SESSION ON COVENANTING AND NAMING

AIM

To enable the group to look at the factors necessary for it to become a community, and to commit themselves to these conditions.

MATERIALS

- Yarn ball for "Yarn Web" (page 12)
- Four children's puzzles, 100-150 pieces
- Large poster board
- Magic marker
- Materials for signing the covenant
- Bible
- Music for "Isaiah 49" by Carey Landry

REMOTE PREPARATION

Appropriate for any group beginning the process of community development.

1. Read the entire lesson carefully, especially the background.

2. You will be dividing into groups of six to nine people. Prepare a work space for each group. At each place, put one of the puzzles. Empty the pieces into a pile, keep three or four in the box, and hide the box.

3. Read through the "Yarn Web" activity (page 12). It makes an excellent icebreaker for a new community.

4. Choose a symbol and prayer ritual for use in the leaders' community. You will be using this throughout the pilot process, to model for the leaders how to use symbol and ritual in their own communities. Rituals and Icebreakers will offer some ideas and guidelines for setting this up.

5. Decide how you will have people sign the covenant: thumbprints, tracing hands, signatures, etc. This will depend on the ages of the children in your group.

OPENING

1. Meet each person at the door. Make sure you know the names of all the family members.

2. Begin by having all persons introduce themselves and share something about themselves with the group.

3. Play the yarn game (10 min.). After playing, take a moment to explain to the the importance of icebreakers. There is a danger of wanting to get to the "meat" of the lesson too soon. If it is clearly understood that the focus is on the development of community, the icebreaker is less apt to be viewed as a frill.

PRAYER (10 MIN.)

1. Explain to the leaders the purpose of the opening ritual, the use of symbols, and the importance of prayer in family faith formation.

2. Celebrate the ritual.

EXPERIENCE

1. Begin by breaking into intergenerational groups. Assign the groups to their work stations and instruct them to put the puzzles together. Do not let them know that some pieces are missing.

2. After approximately ten minutes, give the groups the pictures.

3. In another five minutes supply the missing pieces.

4. Have the group reassemble when the puzzles are done.

EXPLANATION

1. Ask the groups, "What made it easy to put the puzzles together? What made it difficult?" Relate the answers to things that help and hinder the development of community. For example, some helps might be: finding the edges (knowing the limits), having a picture (a model to go by). Some hindrances: pieces missing (people who don't come), people hogging the pieces and not sharing, etc.

2. Like putting the puzzle together, there are certain things that can help a community come together. Explain that the members of the group will be making an agreement with each other to foster the development of the community. Because it is not just an agreement with each other, but also with God, it is called a covenant.

3. Put covenant on the top of the poster board. Ask the group to offer ideas on the things they will need to do if this new community is going to work. Use everyone's ideas. Part of learning to work in an intergenerational community is validating the contributions of each member. It is important for you, as director, to model that for the leaders.

4. Explain to the group that they all will be asked to sign the covenant in the closing prayer.

CLOSING

1. Begin your closing prayer with the refrain to "Isaiah 49."

2. "Loving God,
   we ask you to bless this covenant.
   Help all of us to keep the promises
   we have made.
   Unite us in your love.
   We pray for the N... family."

3. As you pray for each family, invite them forward to sign the covenant. Have gentle music playing in the background. When everyone has signed the covenant, join hands and say the Lord's Prayer, and close with song.

The evening ends with refreshments. Distribute the background sheet for families to take home.

BACKGROUND: COVENANTING AND NAMING

Is there any one of us who can ignore a rainbow when we see one? And when we see one, what is the first thought that runs through our heads? Perhaps notions about white light being split up by particles of water in the air, or a sense of God's hand, God's presence, God's promise....

When it happens to me, typically on a drive down an interstate highway, it usually is a mixture of both thoughts. But soon after, I usually hear a jingle in my head from somewhere in my past, "A rainbow makes a promise that life is here to stay," followed by, "I wish to be a rainbow and promise life to you."

This thought comes from God's promise to Noah after the great flood, when God said, "I have set my bow in the clouds, and it shall be a sign of the covenant between me and the earth.... When the bow is in the clouds, I will see it and remember the everlasting covenant between God and every living creature of all flesh that is on the earth" (see Genesis 9:12-17).

Covenant is the biblical term for the promises and agreement between God and the "chosen people." The primary covenant is the one made with Moses at Sinai (see Exodus 19). It is an agreement between lesser and greater parties (see Exodus 20; CCC 2056). God is faithful, while Israel is unfaithful: God is forever merciful, even when Israel rejects the covenant again and again (CCC 709). God's promise stands forever and moves us to respond in faith and prayer (CCC 2570-74).

A covenant celebrates a personal relationship and the commitment to keep it. We do it daily: We are committed to love and care for our children and our spouses, and we put our whole person into that relationship by being both just and compassionate.

It is also a communal relationship, where I identify with and commit myself to a group of believers, a Church, in the solidarity of sharing faith through justice and compassion. Being together in this way, we are promises of life to one another.

We are all more faithful when our commitment is clearly spelled out. Covenant conveys that we need to remain faithful to each other, even in the face of discouragement and faithlessness, just as God is faithful to us. What we are celebrating are the conditions for becoming a community of faith (CCC 2787, 2790).

Likewise, it is important to give each of our groups a name. What's in a name? Well, somehow, we are. Without a name, the groups tend to refer to themselves by their leader's name: "I'm in Kathy Chesto's group." This places ownership of and responsibility for the group on the leader alone. Calling the group by name gives everyone ownership and responsibility. I wish to be a rainbow and promise life to you.

* *"Rainbow,"* copyright © 1973 by Damean Music. Used by permission of GIA Publications, Inc., Chicago, Illinois, exclusive agent. All rights reserved. Used with permission.

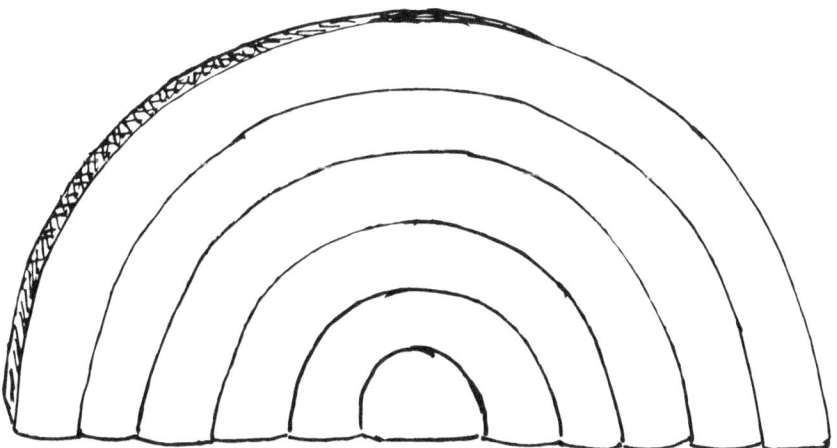

GENERAL COVENANT BLESSING

OVERVIEW

Various themes are provided, with a brief explanation of situations in which these readings, songs, homilies would be particularly appropriate. Those not using a symbol can simply omit the blessing from the general covenant celebration.

BECOMING COMMUNITY

Appropriate for any group beginning the process of community development.

1. Music suggestions:
    - Entrance: "Gather Your People" by Bob Hurd
    - Response: "We Are Many Parts" by Marty Haugen or "Song of the Body of Christ" by David Haas
    - Recessional: "They'll Know We Are Christians" by Peter Scholtes, or "Companions on the Journey by Carey Landry

2. Prayer: **"Loving God, we come to you, seeking to know you through one another, through these small communities you have called your own. Open our eyes and our hearts, to see and know your presence. Teach us wisdom and love. We ask this, as we ask all things, in the name of Jesus, our brother."**

3. First reading: 1 Corinthians 12:12-21

4. Gospel reading: John 1:35-39

5. Homily idea: The celebrant or director of the group explains the connection to answering Jesus' call to "come and see" who he is and where he lives. Ask the group to respond to what that means. What do they expect to learn? Why did Jesus invite the disciples to his home? Why do we meet in homes?

    Like the disciples, we are not making this journey alone. We are dependent on one another. For this reason, we have entered into the process of making a solemn covenant with one another. The community is invited to think quietly about what they are going to do.

CELEBRATING COMMUNITY

Appropriate for any groups studying sacraments or families entering into sacramental preparation.

1. Music suggestions:
   - Entrance: "Anthem" by Tom Conry
   - Response: "All I Ask of You" by Gregory Norbert
   - Recessional: "Anthem" by Tom Conry or "Table of Plenty" by Dan Schutte

2. Prayer: "**Loving God, we come to you, seeking to know you through one another, and through the symbols that are the signs of our Catholic family. Open our eyes and our hearts, to see and know your presence, both in one another and in the rituals we celebrate. Teach us wisdom and love. We ask this as we ask all things, in the name of Jesus, our brother.**"

3. First reading: Ephesians 3:14-21

4. Gospel reading: Luke 14:13-35

5. Homily idea: Celebrant addresses the fact that we are focusing on how we respond to God through sign and symbol. Like the disciples on the road to Emmaus, it is often through our symbols that we come to know the Lord.

THE RESPONDING COMMUNITY

Appropriate for those groups studying salvation history or doing a Bible study on one or more of the books of the Hebrew Testament.

1. Music suggestions:
   - Entrance: "All the Ends of Earth" by Dan Schutte, or any song that proclaims the greatness of God's deeds in history.
   - Response: "Blest Be the Lord" by Dan Schutte, or a song known to the community.
   - Recessional: "All the Ends of the Earth" by Dan Schutte

2. Prayer: "**Loving God, we come to you, seeking to know you through one another and through our Hebrew ancestors' faith in you. Open our eyes and our hearts, to see and know your presence, both in one another and in the story of your actions in the life of the chosen people. Teach us wisdom and love. We ask this as we ask all things, in the name of Jesus, our brother.**"

3. First reading: Genesis 12:1-3

4. Gospel reading: Matthew 5:17-19

5. Homily idea: Celebrant addresses the fact that the history of the "chosen people" is our history, and if we want to know who we are as a Christian family, we need to understand where we came from and how our ancestors came to know God.

THE BELIEVING COMMUNITY

Appropriate for those groups studying the creed or preparing for confirmation.

1. Music suggestions:
   - Entrance: "City of God" by Dan Schutte
   - Response: "Change Our Hearts" by Rory Cooney
   - Recessional: "If God Is For Us" by Grayson Warren Brown

2. Prayer: "**Loving God, we come to you,
   seeking to know you through one another,
   through these small communities
   you have called your own.
   Open our eyes and our hearts,
   so we can understand better
   who you are and what we believe.
   Teach us wisdom and love.
   We ask this, as we ask all things,
   in the name of Jesus, our brother.**"

3. First reading: Colossians 3:12-15

4. Gospel reading: Matthew 7:21-27

5. Homily idea: Celebrant addresses the fact that the group is focusing on what we believe as a Catholic community. The homilist should take a moment to explain that "believe," in this case, does not simply mean "accept the fact." The "I believe" in our creed comes from the Latin "credo," which is literally to "set one's heart on." The words of the creed are the facts we set our hearts on and live by.

THE LIVING COMMUNITY

Appropriate for groups studying the Beatitudes or the commandments, or for Bible study groups focusing on the fifth chapter of Matthew's Gospel.

1. Music suggestions:
   - Entrance: "Beatitudes" by Darryl Ducote
   - Response: "Change Our Hearts" by Rory Cooney, or any song known to the community.
   - Recessional: "Lead Me, Lord" by John D. Becker

2. Prayer: "**Loving God, we come to you,
   seeking to know you through one another
   and to live according to that knowledge.
   Open our eyes and our hearts,
   to see and know your presence,
   and to be your presence
   for others in the world.
   Teach us wisdom and love.
   We ask this as we ask all things,
   in the name of Jesus, our brother.**"

3. First reading: Deuteronomy 6:4-9

4. Gospel reading: Matthew 5:1-12

5. Homily idea: Homilist addresses the group's focus on what it means to live our lives as Catholic Christians. We will look at how the coming of the reign of God depends on each of us truly living Matthew's Gospel, particularly the Sermon on the Mount.

COVENANT CELEBRATION

MATERIALS

- Bowl of water
- Evergreen branch for blessing
- Bible
- Covenants
- Small pieces of cardboard
- Materials for signing the covenant
- Taped reflective music and a way to play it
- Music and music leader
- Symbol for each community (if you plan to use a symbol during this year)

REMOTE PREPARATION

1. Make a small sign for each of the groups/classes that will be participating in the celebration. Put signs on pews or chairs to reserve the space for each group to sit together.

2. Determine how your groups will sign the covenant. If there are many children involved who are not old enough to write their names, you may want to do thumbprints or trace hands. With thumbprints, you will need at least four ink pads for each of the "signing stations," sheets big enough for tracing hands and signing, as well as magic markers for each station.

3. Place a table in front of the altar for the covenants, water, branch, and symbols for each group (if used). The leaders are responsible for bringing the group symbol and covenants written by their groups to the church, with their own names attached to the top.

4. Designate four areas at the edge of the sanctuary for the signing of covenants. They will be signed four groups at a time. Give each leader one of the areas in which they will meet their group to sign, and if there are more than four groups, give them the "wave" they will be in.

5. Walk through the entire celebration with your leaders/teachers, and provide them with copies.

6. Prepare readers for the Scripture, preferably people of different ages.

7. Make a list of leaders' names for the celebrant.

8. Prepare someone to lead the music. Let any music ministers know the date well in advance.

EXPERIENCE

Entrance

Celebrant: "**May the peace of God be with you.**"

All: "**And with your spirit.**"

Use the following components from one of the individual theme options found in the "General Covenant Blessing" starting on page 144.

- Prayer
- First reading
- Response
- Gospel
- Reading
- Homily

Pause

Blessing: Celebrant lifts up the covenants, raising them to heaven:
"**Lord, bless these covenants,
signs of our commitment to you
and to one another.
Enable us to be faithful,
as you are faithful.**"
Celebrant places the covenants back on the table and sprinkles them with holy water, saying:
"**In the name of the Father, and of the Son, and of the Holy Spirit.**"

Response: "**Amen.**"

Blessing: Celebrant lifts up one of the symbols, saying:
"**Lord, bless these symbols,
signs of our commitment,
signs of our belonging to
a community of ritual.
Teach us to celebrate your love.**"
Celebrant sprinkles the symbols with water, saying:
"**In the name of the Father, and of the Son, and of the Holy Spirit.**"

Response: "**Amen.**"

Celebrant: "**I now invite your leaders
to come forward.**"

The leaders come forward and stand in a semicircle before the celebrant:

Celebrant: "**You have been called to act as pastors
to your small flock.
Do you promise to be faithful
to this call?**"

Leaders: "**We do.**"

Celebrant: "**Will you pray for the families**(/children/adults) **in your care?**"

Leaders: "**We will.**"

Celebrant: "**Will you prepare prayerfully and diligently?**"

Leaders: "**We will.**"

Celebrant: "**Members of the community,
will you assist your leaders
by being faithful to the covenant
you are about to sign?**"

Community: "**We will.**"

The celebrant places hands on each of the leader's heads:

Celebrant: "**Loving God,
bless these leaders
who are offering themselves
to you and their communities.
Give them understanding
and gentle hearts,
playful spirits,
and patient faithfulness.
Let their lives be a sign
to their families
and their communities
of your great love.**"

Reader: "**We are the body of Christ.
Our lives will never be complete
without one another.
We need the gifts
that each of us bring.
To remind us of that,
we ask the families to come forward,
one at a time,
to your leader
in the front of the church,
to sign the covenant you have made.
As the families are signing,
we invite the community
to pray for one another.**"

Celebrant reads the names of the first four leaders, hands them their covenants, and invites their communities to come forward. Families come forward, as the reader directed, one at a time.

It may make it easier to have the leaders call the families forward by name. While families are coming forward and signing the covenant, have soft, reflective music playing in the background.

Celebrant: "**As a sign of our commitment,
let us stand and say the prayer that
Jesus taught us.**"

All: The Lord's Prayer (for "The Believing Community" theme, the Apostles Creed should be used here. In this case, the celebrant will say: "**As a sign of our commitment, let us stand and profess our faith.**")

Closing Song: Any song about community that is well known by the group.

BIBLIOGRAPHY

Bell, Catherine. *Ritual Theory, Ritual Practice*. New York: Oxford University Press, 1992.

Benson, Jeanette and Hilyard, Jack L. *Becoming Family*. Winona, MN: St. Mary's College Press, 1978.

Covert, Anita and Thomas, Gordon L. *Communication, Games and Simulations*. Salem, OR: Eric Clearinghouse, 1978.

DeGidio, Sandra. *Enriching Faith through Family Celebrations*. Mystic, CT: Twenty-Third Publications, 1989.

Dillistone, F.W. *The Power of Symbol in Religion and Culture*. New York: Crossroad, 1986.

Forbess-Greene, Sue. *The Encyclopedia of Icebreakers*. Applied Skills Press, 1983.

Foster, Elizabeth Sabrinsky. *Energizers and Icebreakers: For All Ages and Stages*. Minneapolis: Educational Media Corp., 1989.

Kraus, Richard G. *The Family Book of Games*. Hightstown: McGraw-Hill, 1960.

Krueger, Caryl Waller. *1001 Things to Do with Your Kids*. Nashville: Abingdon Press, 1988.

Martos, Joseph. *Doors to the Sacred*. Garden City: Doubleday, 1982.

Meyer, Jerome Sydney. *The Big Book of Family Games: The Most Complete Treasury of Fun-Filled Games and Activities for Family and Friends*. Los Angeles: Galahad Books, 1974.

Peck, M. Scott. *The Different Drum*. New York: Simon and Schuster, 1987.

Ripley, Sherman. *Book of Games*. Chicago: Association Press, 1952.

Stein, Lincoln David. *Family Games*. New York: Macmillan, 1979.

Stuart, Sally E. *100 Plus Party Games: Fun and Easy Ideas for Parties & Holidays*. Santa Fe, Bear & Co., 1988.

Winter, Miriam Therese. *God With Us: Resources for Prayer and Praise*. Nashville: Abingdon, 1979.

Wiswell, Phil. J Hate. *Charades and 49 Other New Games*. New York: Sterling Publishers, 1981.

More Resources from The Pastoral Center & Growing Up Catholic

Why Coach Parents? Resource Kit - FREE

LEARN HOW WHOLE FAMILY CATECHESIS CAN TRANSFORM YOUR PARISH

This versatile kit gives you exactly what you need to help your leaders understand and become excited about a coaching parents approach. And we offer it as our gift to you!

These are the ideal resources for you to use within your parish or school to begin the process of shifting from "doing it for them" to "coaching them to do it themselves." The "it" here is forming their own kids with the faith of the church: passing that faith on to the next generation.

Learn more at http://pastoral.center/family-catechesis-planning

Growing Up Catholic Sacramental Preparation

A WHOLE FAMILY APPROACH THAT COACHES PARENTS

This carefully tested and well-crafted process was designed to coach parents to share faith with their children. This handout-based resource helps parents teach their own children in a parish process, with the support of catechist leaders. Help parents understand their role in forming their children and bringing faith home!

It is available in English & Spanish, and for use with both elementary & middle school children.

Learn more at http://pastoral.center/guc-sacramental-prep

More Whole Family Catechesis Resources...

VISIT OUR WEBSITE TO FIND MANY TOOLS TO HELP YOU FORM FAMILIES

- Seasonal resources to help families prepare for and live through the liturgical seasons and feasts.
- Whole family sessions with easy step-by-step handouts for parents to follow.
- Activity-based lessons well-suited for whole family learning centers.
- Small group resources for parent conversations on topics of family and faith.
- Concise, relevant take-home resources for parents.

Learn more at http://pastoral.center/family-catechesis

www.ingramcontent.com/pod-product-compliance
Lightning Source LLC
Chambersburg PA
CBHW081203240426
43669CB00039B/2796